ys
:);
n-
.i,
n-
n-

's
.st
ay'
'e-
h.
.y,
.!
.n.
he
ter

.h.e
Di-
en-
ing
not
.ing
; to
and

.nce
.ant
/ to
uesr

NATIONAL. MUSEUM,
OF. ROME..
IN. THE. BATHS. OF. DIOCLETIAN

❧❧❧

GUIDE

By. L. MARIANI. and D. VAGLIERI.

ROME

SPOLETO
Premiata Tipografia dell'Umbria
1900

The National Museum of Rome contains antiquities which are the property of the State, and which have been found chiefly in the city and suburbs. It occupies the buildings which once belonged to the stately Convent of the Carthusian brothers of Santa Maria degli Angeli, to whom Pope Pius IV and the Roman people granted the ruins of the Baths of Diocletian on Aug. 5th. 1561, because the convent then occupied by them at Santa Croce in Gerusalemme was inconvenient.

The Hon. Guido Baccelli was the first who thought of turning the cloister into a museum. This idea occurred to him in 1882, but it was little more than a storehouse till 1889, when during the ministry of Boselli it was arranged and opened to the public by the initiative and under the skilful management of Comm. Barnabei. It was enlarged in 1893. under the ministry of Martini, and the last additions were made in 1895 under the direction, of Baccelli.

The cloister, beautiful in its simplicity, is generally attributed to Michael Angelo, who was the first architect of the adjoining church, and who, it is said, made the design according to which it was constructed. The cloister, the perimeter of which is 320 metri, was built in 1565. (*) It is surrounded by one hundred arches, supported by columns of travertine. The fountain in the centre was constructed in 1695, probably to replace the traditional well of Carthusian cloisters. Around it are four cypresses,

---

(*) On the angular pilaster near te entrance is carved the date MDLXV.

two of which date from the time of the construction of the fountain; the others were planted to substitute two that were uprooted by a hurricane on July 18the 1888.

On the north-west side are six small cells, each once occupied by a friar, who lived in almost perpetual solitude and silence, according to the rule of his order.

In each cell, to the left of the entrance, is a cellar with a wood closet above, and to the right communicating with the cloister is a small window, through which food was passed to the inmate. Above one of these windows was once the following inscription, now lost; *Manducate quæ apponuntur vobis*. A short flight of steps leads to the rooms occupied by the friar, three on the first floor, and three on the second, of various dimensions. Each is provided with a porch leading out into the little garden where there was a small oratory. From this garden, which the friar cultivated with his own hands, an elegant little porch gives access by another door to the rooms.

On the other sides of the cloister there never were cells, but the external architectural lines are similar.

The collection of antiquities, except the few placed near the entrance, occupy the four sides of the cloister, together with the garden, five cells on the north west side, and five small rooms to the right of the entrance, besides fourteen rooms on the upper floor, above two sides of a smaller cloister which belongs to the Blind Asylum Margherita di Savoia.

The following pages describe the most important of the antiquities. (*)

(*) The numbers in red refer to the place in the museum, those in black refer to the inventory, and those in blue to the catalogue.

In this guide the antiquities are taken according to the numbers in red.

ENTRANCE COURT.

In the middle is a large cup-shaped vase, under the edge of which are six Cupids in relief. It once stood in the courtyard of Santa Cecilia in Trastevere. The statues under the portico wearing the toga, roughly carved in travertine, were brought from tombs on the Via Appia.

CORRIDOR.

n. 2. Mosaic pavement with geometrical design, brought from the house excavated in the garden of the Farnesina Villa.

n. 5. Mosaic representing two men (bestiarii) fighting with a tiger. The inscription seems to refer to the festivals held every twentieth year when such combats took place. From the Castro Pretorio.

CLOISTER.

1st. SIDE. (S. W.)

No 1 and 3. Statues found in the tomb of the Platorini, (cf. 2nd. Side, nos 13, 19 and 25; upper floor Room II) on the right bank of the Tiber near the Farnesina Villa; they are portraits of persons buried there in the time of Tiberius. The male figure is in Greek heroic costume.

No 1 stands on a marble cippus found at Porcigliana near Castel Porziano, and was presented to the museum by His Majesty the King. It was dedicated by the Laurenti of the Vicus Augustanus to their patron Elius Liberalis, freedman of the Emperor, who was raised to the rank of decurion, and at Ostia held several offices connected with the food supply of the State. The most noteworthy of these was that of *procurator pugillationis et ad naves vagas*, of which we have no other example. His duty in this capacity problably was to register the ships that arrived at Ostia at irregular intervals, not forming part of the grain fleet.

2. Bust of a youthful Vestal (cf. Room H no 3).

4. Head of Venus or Diana. Found under the foundations of the monument to Victor Emmanuel.

5. Statue broght from the Palatine. A similar statue of the same size was discovered during the recent excavations in the stadium on the Palatine, where it may now be seen. It is a replica of the so-called Ariadne of Dresden, (*Augusteum* XVII) and as the two statues were probably originally placed near one another, we may conclude that they represented nymphs or Muses (Cf. the Terpsichore of the Vatican, Hall of the Muses no. s-17). The style of both belongs to the end of the 4th. century B. C. or to the beginning of the Hellenistic period.

6. Youth, Hellenistic type (Narcissus). Found on the spot where the Teatro Drammatico now stands, near the Colonna Gardens in the Via Nazionale.

7. Statue of a Vestal from the House of the Vestal Virgins in the Forum Romanum (cf. Room H. no. 3.)

8. Lower part of a female figure (Muse?). From the Teatro Drammatico Nazionale.

9. Torso of a statuette, a reproduction of the well-known Diomede of the Museum at Munich, of the school of Polycletus, by some attributed to Silanion (4th century B. C.) or to Cresilas; the hero is represented in the act of carrying off the Palladium, as in the relief in the Palazzo Spada. From the Palatine.

10. Head, portrait of a Roman of the 1st Century of the Empire, problably Germanicus. (Cf. Statue in the Lateran Museum). Found in the Tiber near the Marmorata.

11. Statue of a Genius. The features are of a type frequently employed in representing minor divinities in the form of youths; such as the so-called Eubuleus of Eleusis, and the head incorrectly called Virgil. Found in the villa of Voconius Pollio near Marino.

12. Head of Athena (Minerva). From the Tiber.

13. Statue of Hercules, somewhat archaic type. Cf. the Mastai Hercules (Rotonda of the Vatican Museum. No. 544) the Hercules of Carnuntum ec. From the villa of Voconius Pollio.

14. Head of the so-called Seneca (cf. H Room II no. 8.) From the Kircherian Museum.

15. Head, portrait of a Roman lady of the time of Antoninus Pius. From the monument to Victor Emmanuel.

16. Head of Niobe. From the Palatine.

17. Apollo Pythius with the tripod and the serpent. Found in the villa of Voconius Pollio near Marino. Greek type of the middle of the 4th. Century B. C. Roman workmanship copied from a bronze original. It stands on a base dedicated by the Senate of Fidenae to Marcus Aurelius, in the reign of Antonius Pius in the year 140 A. D.

It was brought from the spot known as the *Serpentara* at the Villa Spada on the Via Salaria, site of the ancient city of Fidenae, which during the imperial period was almost deserted.

18. Head of youth, (athlete) Attic type of the 4th. century, anterior to Lysippus. Found in Piazza Nicosia.

19. Torso of Bacchus or of Ampelos. From the Kircherian Museum.

20. Fragment of statue of a Muse (?). From the Teatro Drammatico Nazionale.

22. Head of Lucius Verus. (b. 130 d. 169 AD) cf. G Room 3 no 1. From the Via Appia.

23. Statue of Hera (Juno) found in the stadium of the Palatine. There is wonderful technical skill displayed in the delicate treatment of the folds of the dress, and the depth of the cutting in the hollows. The goddess is of a type resembling the Hera Barberini in the Rotonda of the Vatican. These two, like several other statues, follow one prototype, perhaps of the school of Phidias, but the imitations tend to degenerate into affectation. This statue belongs to the time of the Antonines, and it is not improbable that according to the fashion of the period, the reigning empress was represented with the attributes of the goddess.

24. Portrait head of Vespasian cf. cell B. Room
1. no. 5. From the Tiber.

25. Head of Artemis (Diana). From the House
of the Vestals.

26. and 27. Lower portions of two statuettes of
Muses (?) From the Teatro Drammatico Nazionale.

28. Statuette of Asklepios (Esculapius) with serpent and *omphalos* cf. 4th. Side no. 40. From the
House of the Vestals.

29. Statue of a Roman lady, probably an empress. Discovered in laying the foundations of the
Offices of the War Ministry.

30. Statuette of Nike (Victory) Doric type. Behind the shoulders are traces of wings. From the
Kircherian Museum.

31. Statue probably of an empress in the attitude of prayer, resembling the so called Pietà of
the Vatican. The arms badly restored do not agree
with this hypothesis; the head, not belonging to this
statue, is a portrait of Lucilla (b. 147, d. 183 A D).
From the Sciarra collection.

On the cippus below observe that the name of
Nero has been effaced for the *damnatio memoriæ*.

33. Torso of a Satyr holding a wine-skin on
his knee in the act of drinking. A fountain figure.

34. Head of Cybele or *Magna Mater*. The goddess wears her usual mural crown and veil. From
the Kircherian Museum.

35. A victorious athlete placing a crown on
his head with his right hand, the left holding a
palm. Peloponnesian type, 5th. century. From the
Via Ostiense.

36. Head of Roman of the Ist. century of the
Empire. From the Via Ardeatina.

37. Nymph with shell; very common Greek idea; cf. 2nd. Side no. 31 and Garden 3rd. Side no. 14. Found at the Corner of Via Venti Settembre and Via Firenze.

38. Portrait head of young Roman of the end of the Ist. century of the Empire.

39. Statue of Tyche (Fortune). With her left hand she holds a cornucopia resting on her shoulder. The dress is in the style usually attributed to this goddess, and is copied from Attic statues of the beginning of the 4th. century B. C. From Ostia.

40. Bust of Geta. (b 189. d. 212 A D). From the site of the Office of the Finance Ministry.

CLOISTER 2nd. SIDE.

Colossal tragic mask. Cf. nos 14 and 15. Marble masks of this kind with open mouths were used as decorations for fountains, or to contain a lamp, or were sometimes placed at the openings of hot air tubes in the calidaria of baths.

1. Corinthian capital, carefully restored, richly ornamented and skilfully carved. Found under the Apollo Theatre near the Pons Ælius on the left bank of the Tiber.

Opposite under the arch, a mass of lead such as those which were brought to Rome, marked with the weight and the name of the place from which they came. Found in the Tiber near the Pons Sublicius.

2. Head of Julia Domna, wife of Septimius Severus. From the Palatine.

3. Portion of the frieze encircling the top of the Mole Adriana. Found in the Tiber at the Castle of

St. Angelo. Observe the workmanship and the broad
and deep modelling intended to be effective from a
distance.

4. Head of Meleager. Cf. the famous statue in
the Vatican after the school of Scopas. From the
Palatine.

5. Statue of Apollo, Hellenistic style. From the
works for the Forte Tiburtino at Porta Furba.

6. Head of Asclepius (Æsculapius) as a youth.
Representations of the beardless Asclepius are rare,
but we know that such was the statue made by
Scopas for Gortyna.

7. Statuette of a nymph wrapped in a mantle.
A fountain figure, Hellenistic style. It is interesting
because the colours with which it was painted are
still tolerably well preserved. From the Prati di Ca-
stello near the Ponte di Ripetta.

It stands on a marble cippus reinscribed under
Constans (337-350 A D) and dedicated to L. Aurelius Avianus Smymachus prefect of the supplies.
Perhaps the ship carved on the right side (from
the corn fleet?) is connected with this office. The
inscription on the left side alluding to the consuls of
the year 284 B. C. refers to a previous destination
of the cippus. From the Palatine.

CELL B.

Contains sculptures brought from Ostia.

Room 1.

1. Cinerary urn. On the front of the bas-relief the struggle beween Ulysses and Diomede for
the possession of the arms of Achilles. Helbig be-

lieves that this relief is imitated from the famous painting with which Timanthes was successful in the competition with Parrhasius.

2. Colossal head of Gordian III (d. 241 AD). In spite of the late period, and the destination of the statue to decorative purposes, it preserves the truthfulness of Roman art.

3. Bust of a Roman of the Ist. century of the Empire. Found in 1897.

4. Colossal head of a youth which was ornamented with a diadem, as proved by the chisel marks on the forehead. It is not a portrait, but an ideal head. The workmanship seems to be of the beginning of the 2nd. century A D.

5. A fine portrait of Vespasian (b 9. d. 79 A D), one of the best preserved in existence.

6. Portrait of a Roman lady of the time of the later Antonines (2nd. and 3rd. centuries A D.)

7. Portrait of a Roman of the 3rd. century A D.

8. Portrait of a Roman, reproducing the features attributed to Clodius Albinus (d. 197 A D) or of Hannibal (cf. Torlonia Museum no 478).

9. Small bust of Marcus Aurelius (b. 122. d. 180 A D). cf. H Room 3 no. 5.

10. Head of Plotina wife of Trajan (b about 109 d. 169 A D).

The altar no. 11 found in the portico, behind the stage of the theatre, is of remarkable beauty. Its sides are decorated with reliefs; that on the front represents Cupid between Mars and Venus with a youth who seems to have the attributes of Mercury (Iulus according to some). on two sides two Cupids are playing with the arms and chariot of Mars. The fourth side is worthy of special notice, because of the relief illustrating the legend of the foundation of Rome. In the lower portion is the wolf in a cavern with Romulus and Remus, near the Tiber, which is represented by a recumbent figure on the right. Above the cavern is the eagle symbolising Rome, and shepherds passing on the right are watching the miracle.

This altar which is remarkable for the delicacy of the carving of the animals and other decorations, was dedicated to Silvanus and other deities by P. Attius Sinerus procurator of Crete, and by his sons 1st. Oct. 124 A D, under the Emperor Hadrian as proved by the inscriptions. P. Attius Sinerus was a freedman of P. Elius Trophimus, himself a freedman of the Emperor. The words *decurionum decreto* must refer to a grant of land.

It is a disputed point whether the sculpture is of the same date as the inscription, which from its ill-adapted position seems to have been added later. Some authorities believe that the altar was executed in the reign of Augustus, from the elegance of the style, and from the fact that on the principal side are carved the divinities of the Julian house. Augustus revived and diffused the worship of these gods to celebrate the new order of things established by him with the Empire. We, however, regard it as belonging to the time of Hadrian, because on the pediments of the temple of Venus and Rome, built by him, were two reliefs analogous to those of this altar, which may perhaps have been erected on the occasion of the dedication of the temple.

Room 2.

Portrait of a Roman of the later republican period or of the early years of the Empire; one of the
best specimens of the skill of Roman sculptors in
reproducing the human physiognomy. It has a certain resemblance to the well-known portrait incorrectly supposed to be Caius Marius.

Room 3.

5. Fine bust of Septimius Severus (b 146. d.
211 A. D.) According to some, Pertinax.

1. 3.' 4 and 6. Small columns of bigio dorato
carved from ancient blocks, and supporting four
elegant marble vases carved in relief.

2. Head crowned; unknown portrait of the
Ist. century of the Empire. Some say a Roman empress; in our opinion it may possibly represent a
eunuch, priest of Cybele.

7. Head of youth (a priest?) wearing a circlet
ornamented with two plaques on which are carved
busts of divinities. According to some, Antinous.

Loggia.

1. Sleeping nymph.

2nd. SIDE.

10. Head in the style of the Athena Giustiniani.
(Vatican, Braccio Nuovo no. 114.) Of the latter half
of the 5th. century or beginning of the 4th. B C;
sometimes attributed to the sculptor Euphranor.
From the Kircherian Museum.

11. Fragment of frieze decorated with olive branches, an eagle and a mask, from a circular building. Found in the stadium of the Palatine; probably part of the temple of Apollo.

Opposite, under the arch a male torso, archaic. From the Tiber.

12. Another head of Minerva, or according to some, of a hero or of Mars. Style of the middle of the 4th. century B. C.

Found in the Tiber near the Marmorata.

13. Inscription carved *in opera* from the tomb of the Platorini. (Cf. Ist. Side, nos 1 and 3, 2nd. Side, nos 19 and 25, upper floor Room II). The surface of the slab is curved so as to make the border stand out like a frame. It is in memory of the wife of Q. Marcius Barea Sura, Antonia Furnilla, who must have been the mother of Marcia Furnilla second wife of Titus, and mother of Julia.

CELL C.

Near the door is placed a fragment of a replica of the so-called Artemis Colonna of the Museum of Berlin and of that of the Vatican (Braccio Nuovo no. 92). The style resembles that of Praxiteles. The goddess is walking in haste, and her floating robes clinging to her figure reveal its outlines.

In this and the next cell is a remarkable epigraphic collection, containing the records of the Arval brothers. To this collection we owe the ample knowledge we possess of this brotherhood, a knowledge more complete than we have of any other institution, whether sacred or secular, of ancient Rome. The greater number of these fragments were found between the years 1867 and 1871 in the vineyard of Ceccarelli, now belonging to Jacobini, on the site of the sacred grove of the Arvales, *via Campana apud lapidem quintum,* whence at an early period they were transferred to other parts of the city and suburbs. Every year in the month of April or of May the records of the confraternity were carved on marble tablets which were preserved in a temple. The few in plaster in this collection are copies of those existing in other museums.

The last tablet discovered refers to the year 241 A D. It is probable that about that time the imperial protection was withdrawn, and the wealth and importance of the confraternity came to an end, together with the custom of carving the records on marble.

We have many proofs of the great antiquity of the confraternity; first we have the song to whch the brothers danced *à trois temps* which is preserved in the records of the year 218; « *Enos Lases juvate, enos Lases juvate, enos Lases juvate! neve luerve (luem ruem ?) Marmar sins (sinas ?) incurrere in pleores (=plures), neve luerve Marmar sins incurrere in pleores, neve luerve Marmar sins incurrere in pleores! satur fu, fere Mars! limen sali, sta berber! satur fu, fere Mars! limen sali, sta berber! satur fu, fere Mars! limen sali sta berber! semunis (=Semones) alternei advocapit (advocabitis ?) conctos, semunis alternei advocapit conctos, semunis alternei advocapit conctos! Enos Marmor juvato, enos Marmor juvato, enos Marmor juvato! Triumpe, triumpe, triumpe, triumpe, triumpe!* » This song, the meaning of which was not clear to the priests who sang it, and still less to the stonemason who carved it on the marble, is most obscure to us, but it undoubtedly referred to the Lares (*Lases*) and to Mars (*Marmar, Marmor*).

The exclusion of iron from the sanctuary is another proof of antiquity. This exclusion was so absolute as to require expiatory sacrifices *ob ferrum inlatum in aedem* or *de aede elatum scripturæ causa*. A third proof is the use of handmade vessels. The ne *Dea Dia* venerated by the brotherhood, and unknown to us from any other source, points to a time when deities were known by an attribute rather than by their names. This goddess was evidently connected with the sowing of seed.

The Arval year began with the Saturnalia, between the nones and ides of January. At that time, the *magister* or president of the confraternity announced in solemn form, *manibus lautis velato capite sub divo columine contra orientem*, the days of the festivals of the goddess, which usually were the 17th., 19th., and 20th., or 27th., 29th. and 30th of May (cf. records of the year 91). These festivals are specially described in the records of the year 218.

On the first day at dawn in the house of the *magister*, after a sacrifice of incense and wine, the brethren consecrated *fruges aridæ et virides et panes laureati*, and anointed the image of the goddess; in the afternoon they met for a banquet, and before the *mensa altera* they again offered to the goddess wine and incense, then having distributed among themselves wreaths, roses, confectionery, and to each person a sportula (small basket) containing 100 denarii, they separated with the salutation, *felicia*. On the second day they met in their grove after the sacrifice of two young pigs (*porcae piaculares*) and

of a cow by the *magister*, to offer an *agna opima*
in the temple; then having placed the viscera of the
animals in the tetrastylum, a building at the foot of
the hill, the *magister* signed the record and retired.
Towards noon all met in the tetrastylum to eat the
pigs, then all present, having put on the toga prae-
texta, *capite velato, vittis spiceis coronati* (the
white fillet and the crown of wheat-ears which were
the badges of these priests) they went up into
the wood to sacrifice a sheep, and to offer the usual
wine and incense. Then within the temple was made
a *sacrum ollis*, the meaning of which is not known,
while a similar offering was made outside by the
magister and the *flamen*; finally, having placed a
sum of money on the altar, all went out. Two of
the number went to fetch the *fruges aridae et vi-
ridae* consecrated on the previous day, which were
passed from one to another. Re-entering the temple, they addressed a prayer to the vessels of meal,
which were then thrown down on the roadway.
Then all seated themselves while the *panes laure-
tani* were brought, and the statues of goddesses (it
is evident, that more than one is meant) were
anointed. All strangers were then obliged to go out,
and the doors were shut, while the brethren reading
the words from a book, danced and sang the song
before-mentioned. Then they crowned the goddess,
and proceeded to nominate the *magister* and *flamen*
for the coming year, again closing the ceremony
with the word *felicia*. After a banquet with the dis-
tribution of roses and *sportulae*, there were races
in the circus.

On the third day the brethren met at the house
of the *magister* at another banquet with various cere-

monies, and the festivals concluded with cheers for
the emperor.

There were many other expiatory sacrifices
which are worthy of remark as a further proof of
the antiquity of the confraternity.

The true reason why Augustus reorganised this
institution and revived the ancient ceremonies is to
be found in another of its functions which has no
connection with those already described. The Arvals
were expected to make vows and sacrifices for the
benefit of the emperor and his family on various
occasions, and at the beginning of every year they
vowed *pro salute et incolumitate imperatoris*, and
of his family a series of sacrifices to be made to
several divinities. They also offered sacrifices on the
accession of an emperor, for the dignitaries, for restoration to health, for the safe delivery of the empress, for the births in the family for safe return from
a journey etc. Thus the records of the Arval brotherhood are of immense value as being a chrono-
logy of the Empire.

To the left of the entrance in cell C. is placed
the only portion yet discovered of the calendar of
the Augustan period, which was kept in the sacred
grove of the confraternity, and which contained a
list of the public festivals, not only those peculiar
to the Arvals. From the numerous abrasions it is
plain that the calendar was corrected on the intro-
duction of new festivals.

In the middle of the first room is the altar of
travertine which was placed in the sacred grove. It
is decorated with bucrania and encarpa, with the
serpent representing the *Genius loci*.

Porch

A beautiful fragment of sculpture representing a woman seated. Observe the arrangement of the drapery, and the traces of polychrome treatment.

The sarcophagus standing near with many confused figures is a work of the time of Septimius Severus or Caracalla, as may be seen by the style of hair-dressing of the deceased woman, whose bust is represented. In the middle is Bacchus surrounded by his cortège (thiasos) and leaning on a satyr; around are shepherds, Cupids and other figures intent on various field labours.

CLOISTER 2nd SIDE.

16. Head, portrait of a Greek woman (according to Helbig a priestess) attributed to the second half of the 5th. century on which Furtwaengler recognises the influence of Calamis in the style. From the Kircherian Museum.

17. Venus *Anadyomene*. It preserves traces of polychrome treatment, especially in the hair which is red, perhaps as a preparation for gilding.

18. Head of king or general, Hellenistic style, wearing a Phrygian helmet.

19. Marble slab which was built into the wall over the architrave above the door of the tomb discovered in 1880 between the wall of Aurelian and the Ponte Sisto (cf. Ist. Side nos 1, 3; 2nd. Side, nos 13, 25; upper floor Room II.) The Sulpicius Platorinus mentioned in the inscription was probably nephew of the man of the same name who was triumvir of the mint in the year of Rome 736. Sul-

picia Platorina, wife of Cornelius Priscus, seems to have been the sister of the triumvir.

20 and 21. Two heads of heroes found near the tomb of the slaves and freedmen of the Statilii near Porta Maggiore. The first, wearing the χυνέη or leather helmet, is according to some authorities, Ulysses; according to others, an idealised portrait of the 4th. century B. C., perhaps of a barbarian. The other is a heroic portrait (?) of the time of Gallienus.

CELL D.

In the middle of the first room stands a pedestal in the form of an altar with delicate relief, found on the bank of the Tiber where once stood the Apollo Theatre.

On the walls are exhibited the tablets of the Arval records in continuation of those of Cell C. On the left of the entrance is a tablet containing the series of Roman magistrates from the year 2 B. C. to 37 A. D.

Room 2.

Bronze tablet found in the district known as the *Macchia di Reino* near Circello on the left bank of the river Tamaro (province of Beneventum) where once stood the city of the Baebian Ligures. It was taken from a curia, basilica or temple in the Forum, and sent to Campolattaro, then by direction of the late minister the Hon. Ruggiero Bonghi, placed in the Kircherian Museum, and thence sent here. This tablet refers to a contract by which private individuals were enabled to borrow a portion of the sum appointed by the emperor from the treasury to supply corn or money to the children of poor Roman citizens. The borrowers gave as security a certain amount of landed property inferior in value to the sum borrowed. The tablet contains a register of these securities for the archives of the city with the following particulars; 1. name of the borrower; 2. name of the land given as security and its exact position; 3. sum borrowed; 4. value of the land and amount of the interest at $2^1/_2$ per cent paid half yearly.

In the same room are collected some fragments of the records of the ludi saeculares (cf, upper floor Room I nos 1 and 2) and some restored portions of pavements richly inlaid with coloured marble (opus sectile) from the palace of Caligula on the Palatine.

Room 3.

In the middle, Hermes (Mercury.) From the combination of various styles in this statue it may be conjectured that it is one of the eclectic works done in Rome by Greek artists of the Ist. century of the Empire, whose practice was to combine the styles of various epochs. This was the principle adopted by the school of Pasiteles. In the pose of this statue we recognise the style of Lysippus, the head is Attic of the early part of the 4th. century, and the archaic treatment of the hair and beard recalls Polycletus.

Furtwaengler supposes that it is a youthful work of Scopas. The use of a streaked bluish Greek marble is peculiar. Found on the Palatine.

1. Marble cippus dedicated to L. Julius Vehilius Gratus Julianus praetorian prefect, put to death by

Commodus, and thrown into the piscina, as related by the biographer of that Emperor. It is important as giving the series of honours enjoyed by Julianus during a period of nearly thirty years (161-189), and particularly as describing the part he took in the dangerous wars of the reigns of M. Aurelius and Commodus. But its chief value is that it serves to prove that the last book of the Periegesis of Pausanias was written after the year 179, because that author says that in his time the Castaboci were driven as far as Elatea in Phocis, giving the date of that event in accordance with this inscription as 178-179.

2. Marble slab presented by Count Tyszkiewicz, and evidently found on the Via Ostiense. It contains two letters referring to a concession of ground for the construction of a tomb. A certain Geminius Eutichetes who rented some market gardens on the Via Ostiense the property of the *collegium magnum arcarum divarum Faustinarum Matris et Piae* having always paid his rent regularly, begs the quinquennial officer Salvius for permission to construct in those gardens a small sepulchral monument twenty feet square, with an approach and a space round it. On the second division of the slab is a letter from the quinquennials dated 25th. July 227 A. D. advising the quaestors and scribes of the association that the concession has been made, and warning them to take care that Eutichetes does not occupy a larger space than that for which he has asked. There are but few *libelli* of a similar character in existence; besides this only two are known; viz. that of Adrastus now in the Vatican Museum, and that of Vesbinus in the Museum of Naples.

3. Cippus of travertine found in 1873 in an old wall near the offices of the Finance Ministry. It refers to a contract for work in the Via Caecilia, and is important as giving the name and direction of the road, which was a ramification of the Via Salaria. It belongs to the republican period, probably to the time of Sylla.

In the loggia of this cell are three bases of travertine from the temple of Jupiter Capitolinus, with epigraphic fragments belonging to a series of deeds which after the Mithridatic war were placed in the Capitol by the ambassadors of those Asiatic nations with whom the Romans had concluded treaties of alliance. They were found in the Piazza della Consolazione in 1886.

Porch.

Christian sarcophagus of the end of the 4th. century or beginning of the 5th., found during the demolition of the cloister of San Giacomo in Settimiana near the Farnesina.

It derives importance from the numerous representations of scenes in the lives of Christ, of Moses and of St. Peter.

On the left is Moses in the act of bringing forth water from the rock, then an apostle with a scroll, and St Peter as a prisoner. Then come the miracles of the marriage at Cana, and the multiplication of the loaves and fishes; in the centre is a figure at prayer, symbolising the departed, then the healing of a blind man, the prediction to St Peter of his denial, the resurrection of Lazarus, and Mary Magdalene or Martha at the feet of Christ.

On the front of the cover to the left, are the manger, the healing of the woman who touched Christ's garment, the sacrifice of Isaac, and Moses receiving the tables of the law. To the right in the midst of scenes of rural life which represent the reward of good works, is a canopy under which is a half length figure of the departed, whose epitaph is carved on the central tablet; *Luc. M. Claudiano viro perfectissimo qui vixit plus minus annis XLIII deposito VIII kalendas Decembres in pace.*

CLOISTER 2nd SIDE CONTINUED.

22. Portrait of a Roman of the 4th century A. D.

23. Venus *Anadyomene* From the works on the Tiber near the Ponte di Ripetta. It stands on a cippus dedicated to Julius Asper, consul in 212. A. D.)

24. Head of a Greek, (end of 5th Century B. C. Perhaps an iconical portrait of Sophocles anterior to the statue in the Lateran Museum. From the Palatine.

25. Slab in three pieces belonging to the tomb of Sulpicius Platorinus, (see no. 19) but not found in its original position. It refers to a governor of a province under Tiberius and Caligula, and to his wife Crispina, daughter of Caepio, probably the same who was quaestor of Bithynia in the year 15 A. D. The third person named in the inscription is his son Septicius.

CELL E.
Room 1.

Chiefly contains reliefs, some of which are Greek, others replicas of Greek originals.

1. Head of Athena (Minerva) from Monte Melone near Monte Porzio.

2. Fragment of a sarcophagus with reliefs of Tritons and Nereids.

3. Fragment of alto rilievo with a figure of a youth wearing a chlamys (scarf).

4. Head of Zeus (Jupiter) style of Lysippus.

5. Horse beside a pilaster on which is a dolphin (Cf. no 9). Greek bas-relief relating to racing. From the collection of Ricciotti Garibaldi.

6. Bas-relief. Sacrifice to the Lares, one of whom is represented on the left.

7. Idem. Sacrifice.

8. Idem. The most beautiful fragment in this room, in delicacy resembling a cameo. In the two half figures of warriors (perhaps Ulysses and Diomede) in ambush, the expression of anxiety and curiosity is especially remarkable. A Hellenistic work.

9. Idem. Three Cupids racing in the circus (cf. the sarcophagi in the hall of the Biga in the Vatican Museum.) In the background are seen a goal, and a platform with six dolphins, the number of which indicated the number of rounds of the race course, and further still, an obelisk. From the Kircherian Museum.

10. Idem. Fortune, archaistic. (Roman).

11. Fragment of an archaistic relief (Greek) representing Apollo and Artemis. Under the feet of the god is the *omphalos*. Part of the staff with the twisted serpent is to be seen, and in front of the altar are the other attributes of Apollo, also part of the torch of Diana.

12. Fragment of heroic relief of the end of the 4th century B. C.

13. Relief; head of Vestal idealised. From the Palatine.

14. Relief representing Helen with the Dioscuri. From the Kircherian Museum.

15. Fragment of Bacchic relief.

16. Head; copy of a portrait of a Greek woman of the beginning of the 4th century. The hair is bound with a *sphendone* (band). From Monte Melone.

17. Idem. Copy of head of a Greek woman. Style of the end of the 5th century B. C.

18. (Under the window). Fragment of relief of a yonthful head of delicate and exquisite workmanship.

19. Boeotian shield or ancile.

20. Votive bas-relief to Zeus Xenios (Jupiter god of hospitality), according to a Greek inscription dedicated in fulfilment of a promise made because of a dream. The very original style, and some epigraphic peculiarities suggest that it was an archaistic work, that is, an imitation made in the late Hellenistic or Roman period. From the University Collection.

21. Roman relief of great delicacy of execution; a fragment of a sacrificial scene of which nothing remains but a graceful figure of Mercury (Camillus,) and part of another figure; both carry sacrificial utensils, the *praefericulum* (dish) *acerra* (censer) and *patera* (bowl). From the Kircherian Museum.

22. Relief representing Pentheus pursued by the Maenads, somewhat archaistic in style. Presented in 1887 by Sir. J. Savile Lumley, English ambassador. Found in the Jacobini vineyard, Via Portuense.

23. Fragment in alto-rilievo; the upper part of a dancing figure with an architectural background. Good especimen of Hellenistic sculpture. From the University.

24. Bas relief, front of a small cinerary urn representing a door.

25. Alto-rilievo, fragment of a sarcophagus. A *Gorgoneion* or head of Medusa in Hellenistic style.

26. Fragment of medallion in very low relief, with a Silenus dancing and playing on pipes.

27. Relief, a carriage drawn by two dromedaries and driven by a monkey; a spectacle sometimes exhibited to the public in the circuses of Alexandria and Rome.

28. Alto-rilievo, perhaps a fragment of a sepulchral cippus, with two draped headless female figures.

29. Fragmente of candelabrum with satyr playing on a lute, and a hand of Bacchus holding ont a tankard.

30. (Over the door) Large mask of a river-god, horned. Ornament of a fountain basin. (*labrum*).

Room 2.

The most valuable objects are nos. 3 and 8 found on the Palatine. They belong to a series of reliefs after Phidias representing mythological scenes treated dramatically, whence it has been supposed that they were votive offerings for theatrical successes.

No. 3. is part of a replica of the well known reliefs of the Museum of Naples, and of the Villa Albani, representing Hermes Psychopompos (Mercury guide of souls) leading Eurydice back to Orpheus.

No 8 of which the central figure is partly of
plaster, is a portion of a fragment now in the garden
of the Pigna at the Vatican, and represents, according to Savignoni, the first outbreak of wrath
between Latona and Niobe.

No 9, Prometheus gnawed by the vulture, (found
in the Tiber,) and no 5. representing the philosopher
Anaximander in a pensive attitude are both remarkable, and are in Hellenistic style.

7. Portrait of a Roman woman of the time of
Marcus Aurelius. (2nd century A. D.)

10. Greek sculpture, beginning of 4th century
or end of 5th B. C. It represents a young girl with
melancholy expression, a fragment of a tomb
relief (?)

1. 4 and 6. Architectural ornaments in the form
of thyrsi. From the Palatine.

11. This statuette is one of the most beautiful
reproductions of a well-known Hellenistic type. There
are other examples in the Vatican. (Gallery of the
Candelabra nos 174 and 176, and the Chiaramonti
Museum no 708), in Florence (Magazzino del Museo) Munich, (Glyptothek no 309) and in England
at Wilton House (Kennedy p. 49) It is a satyr, turning to look at his tail, of which he seems to have
only now become conscious. From the Palatine.

Room 3.

3. A pediment on which are represented the
Capitoline divinities, Jupiter, Juno and Minerva, and
two busts of the Dioscuri. From the University.

The Capitoline divinities are roughly repeated
in a block of travertine placed at the entrance of

this cell, on the left side of which are also represented Æsculapius, Hygeia, and Telesphorus the
god of convalescence.

1. This beautiful fragment of a head resembling
fine modern sculpture is the replica of a Hellenistic
type preserved in a bust in Naples and other places;
it perhaps represents a nymph or Muse, though
some of the features suggest a portrait. According
to some, it belongs to the figure of a dancing girl.

Small Room 4.

In this room is a block of stone carved in relief to represent the stage of an ancient theatre.
There are three doors for the three chief actors,
and in the other spaces betwen the columns are
square openings, perhaps for *pinakes* or painted tablets. In the upper part is carved the roof, showing
the panels from below. It is supposed that this
being an isolated piece of carving, was an ex voto
from an actor or builder.

2. Fragment of a relief representing a temple.
The serpent carved on the pediment suggests that
it may be the temple of Æsculapius on the island
of the Tiber.

3. Fragment of relief with a trophy of arms.

4. Fragment of architectural relief with carved
shields.

5. Fragment of a sarcophagus with a procession
of Cupids.

Loggia.

The head of a horse, skilfully carved, is from
Monte Melone (villa of Milo ?) near Monte Porzio,

Nos. 2 and 3. Cippus of greyish tufo with archaic inscriptions (6th century of Rome) found towards the end of 1882 near Palestrina in the vineyard of Soleti. They were dedicated to Hercules, and were intended to support statues.

3. Bust in peperino; Etruscan portrait of the period of the decline of art. The inscription on the mantle bears the words L. CVTHERNAS. LARISAL. CLA(N) that is, *Larte Cuterna son of Larisa* (= *wife of Larte*).

5. Head of a youth, end of 5th century or beginning of 4th B. C.

7. Hellenistic head of Apollo.

8. Head of Minerva or of Rome. From Monte Melone.

P o r c h .

1. Archaistic altar with three goddesses in bas-relief on three sides, and a tripod on the fourth.
From the Via Appia.

2. Fragment of inscription from the tomb of the Platorini. (Cf. 2nd Side nos 13, 19 and 25).

3. Capital of angular Corinthian pilaster, excellent in style. From the Castle of St. Angelo.

4. Small sarcophagus of a child, bad sculpture of the decline of art, but interesting on account of the scenes represented; in the centre Achilles resting on a couch under which is the dead body of Hector; at the sides, the wolf, Cerberus and other figures. These various ideas were apparently not clearly understood by the artist, and he has therefore confused them.

28. Bust of the beginning of the Empire; portrait of an old man, a characteristic example of Roman realistic style which excelled in reproducing individual features. From the Tiber near Ponte Sisto.

29. Fragment of frieze from the Forum of Trajan. Purchased from a dealer in antiquities.

30. Bust which Helbig thinks may represent Hadrian in the early years of his reign. From the Tiber.

31. Nymph with shell. (Cf. Ist. Side no 37.)

CELL F.

Contains various sculptures. To the left of the entrance are placed several copies and Roman reproductions of Attic art of the 4th century B. C.

Room 1.

4. The most beautiful example of the celebrated satyr playing on the flute. This elegant headless statue was found in 1893, when digging for the foundations of the American Episcopal Methodist church in the Via Venti Settembre. The incomplete portions are supplied by the fragment of a replica of the same subject, no. 3, placed near it, which was found in an old wall on the Via Labicana near Tor Pignattara.

5. Part of a group representing Hermes supporting on his hand the little Dionysos entrusted to

his care; the child turns with affection and infant grace, holding out his arms to his protector, who gazes at him tenderly. The idea is similar to that of the Hermes and Dionysos of Praxiteles (at Olympia) and to that of Irene and Plutus of Cephisodotus (at Munich,) though it is not an exact copy of either, and is of a somewhat later period. Klein has reconstructed the group from this statuette and from a statue of Hermes in the Museum at Madrid. Found on the Palatine.

2. Head of Apollo Sauroctonos, replica of another famous statue by Praxiteles cf. other examples in the Vatican (Gall. of statues no 264.) Villa Albani (bronze statuette no. 952) British Museum, Louvre etc. From the Palatine.

6. Beautiful head of Apollo, style of 4th century B. C. From the stadium on the Palatine.

7. Torso of a satyr pouring out liquor. Copy of an original by Praxiteles (cf. Boncompagni Museum no 32.) From the foundations of the monument to Victor Emmanuel.

8. Head, portrait of a Roman of the later republican period.

9. Bust, portrait of a Roman, or perhaps of a barbarian of the beginning of the 3rd century A. D.; very realistic.

10. Very beautiful bust, portrait of a Roman of the 1st century of the Empire.

11. Head of a Cupid; Alexandrian school.

12. Head of a Roman, 1st Century of the Empire.

Room 2.

Observe the graceful head of a woman slightly bent in an attitude of mournful thought, a much injured copy of an excellent work, the so-called Penelope. The best example is in the Vatican Museum (Gallery of statues no. 261) but the original face is wanting.

1. Head of Apollo, style of the end of the 5th century B. C.

3. Head of a youth of the 5th centnry B. C. perhaps *Thanatos* or *Hypnos*. The face which has been added as a restoration to the Penelope of the Vatican is from a replica of this head.

Room 3.

In this room are placed characteristic specimens of the varions styles of hairdressing of the Roman ladies of the imperial period.

7. The complicated fashion of the reign of Augustus as seen in the portraits of Octavia (b. about 60 B. C. d. 11 A. D.) and of Julia (b. 39. B. C. d. 14 A. D.), sister and daughter of the Emperor.

8. Reproduction of the arrangement of the hair in the form of a diadem of curls of the time of the Flavii (= no 9. Room VII cf. no 3. 4th Side).

9. The wig of the time of Matidia, niece of Trajan (1st half of the 2nd century).

10. The style of the time of the elder Faustina (d. 141).

12. The simple hairdressing of the beautiful Sabina wife of Hadrian (b. abont 85. d. about 138 A. D.). (Cf. no 8 Room 1. H and no 10 Room XI).

2. The waving hair of Lucilla wife of Lucius Verus. (b. 147? d. 138 A. D.) (cf. no 8. H. Room 3).

6. The fashion of the reign of Septimius Severus.

1. Portrait of Julia Domna (cf. 2nd Side no 2) with wig, and hair underneath visible.

4. Style adopted by Julia Mammaea (abont 220-230 A. D.).

11. Fashion of the middle of the 3rd century A. D.

5. A specimen of provincial fashion and art, perhaps of the time of Augustus.

Passage no 4.

Specimens of archaic types.

LOGGIA.

Archaic and Egyptian types.

PORCH.

Mosaic with pigmies in boats on the Nile indicated by crocodiles and hippopotami, and the lotus flower. In the little garden of this cell and of that which adjoins it are two colossal heads found in the Tiber under the Castle of St. Angelo.

CLOISTER 2nd SIDE CONTINUED.

35. Artemis, (Diana) very common Hellenistic type. She in clothed as a huntress, and is in the act of shooting an arrow from her bow. From the excavations for the monument to Victor Emmanuel.

36. **Head of a Greek philosopher.** Idealised portrait of Roman execution. According to Helbig, it represents Pythagoras. From the excavations for the monument to Victor Emmanuel.

37. A very important relief. It belongs to another fragment now in the Lateran Museum (Benndorf. — Schoene, Catalogue no 20) which, without the modern restoration, probably represents the Emperor Hadrian, walking in a procession to the temple which he built to Venus and Rome. The part here preserved shows the greater portion of this building with six of the ten columns of its façade. On the pediment is a bas relief relating to the origin of Rome. In the centre reclines Rhea Silvia, and near her Mars (the legs alone and part of the lance preserved), on the left the wolf and the twins, beyond are the shepherds with their flocks, gazing in wonder at the scene. The right side of the relief is wanting. Below, between the columns, are carved the fasces, which were borne by the figures of lictors still lower down.

39. **Statue of a woman in semi-archaistic costume.** It stands on a cippus dedicated to a priestess of the « *dea Virgo Caelestis praesentissimum numen loci montis Tarpei.*» It was discovered in the course of the works for the monument of King Victor Emmanuel, and this fact suggested to Gatti the very probable hypothesis that the name *Ara Coeli* is connected with the *dea Caelestis*, the patroness of Carthage, formerly venerated on this spot.

40. **Bust**, perhaps a portrait of Marcus Aurelius in youth.

41. **Mosaic** found on the Aventine. It represents the inundation of the Nile, with pigmies chasing

hippopotami among other animals and plants of the river. At the beginning of the empire, after the occupation of Alexandria the representation of Egyptian scenes had become fashionable. Cf. the paintings exhibited on the floor above.

CLOISTER 3rd SIDE.

1. Bust of Julius Caesar (?)
2. Cover of sarcophagus of Lucius Julius Athenaeus, a potter. Specimen of Etruscan art in its decline. The sarcophagus on which it rests, but to which it does not belong, bears a relief of Cupids occupied in making weapons; a subject repeated on another sarcophagus placed in the garden side I V no 44.
3. Geta (?) or a personage of his time; (first quarter of 3rd century A. D.).
4. Marble cippus formd in the Bertone vineyard on the Via Praenestina, decorated at the sides with *patera* (bowl) and *praefericulum* (dish).

It was erected by his sons to a certain M. Antonius Terentius of Misenum, who held all the municipal offices in that city, and was in Rome « *negotiator celeberrimus suariae et pecuariae,* » i. e. a famous dealer in pigs and sheep.

5. Portrait of a Roman personage of the time of Antoninus Pius (138-161 A. D.). From Portonaccio.

6 and 14. Marble cippi from the Via Nomentana erected to two brothers, Manius Valerius Saturninus and Manius Valerius Bassus.

7. Bust, according to Helbig a portrait of the Emperor Balbinus (d. 238 A. D.).

8. Sarcophagus on which is represented in relief, on the left a shoemaker at work near a cupboard on which stand two pairs of shoes. Near him another workman is twisting a cord. On the right two figures are performing a religions dance. These two mén, probably freedmen, were named respectively Lucius Atilius Artemas and Titus Fabius Trophimus. The Greek inscription on the tablet says that Lucius Atilius Artemas and his wife Claudia Apphias gave a space in their tomb to their friend T. Fabius Trophimus, who had always lived with them. From the relief it may be inferred that the two freedmen carried on the trades of shoemaker and ropemaker, and were initiated in the mysteries.

11. Bust of a Roman woman of the 3rd century A. D.

13. Septimius Severus (?) cf Cell B Room 3. no 5. and H Room 1 no 6. From the Kircherian Museum.

17. Head, according to Helbig an idealised portrait of the Hellenistic period. The person is represented under the form of νέος Διόνυσος and had therefore on his forehead two little horns the holes for which may still be seen. The successors of Alexander desired to be regarded as divinities (cf Room XII no. 10). According to some it represents Dionysos as Meleager.

18. Front of a large Roman sarcophagus of the 3rd. century from the Via Appia. In the middle are a husband and wife united by Juno Pronuba,

and at the sides the Dioscuri, with personifications of a river, and of the Earth.

19. Portrait of a Roman of the time of Marcus Aurelius. From the Septizonium.

21. Bust of a Roman of the end of the Republic or the beginning of the Empire. — From the Tiber. — Column of verde antico.

22. Idem of the time of the Antonines. — From Ostia. — Column of porta-santa.

23. Roman portrait of the republican period, said to be of Scipio Africanus. A reproduction of the style of the bust of the Capitoline Museum (no. 49.) and not of the Rospigliosi head in basalt. Several antique heads, of old men show a scar on the bald portion; one savant thinks that such portraits were offered by freedmen to their masters in remembrance of their manumission, and that the scar symbolises the stroke of the rod at the act of liberation. Cf. upper floor Room VIII no. 10.

24. A Roman sarcophagus from San Nereo with a relief of Bacchus finding Ariadne at Naxos. The god has descended from his chariot to admire the beauty of the sleeping maiden whom Eros (Love) shows to him; around them is the *thiasos* or cortège of Bacchus.

25. The so called Marcus Brutus, similar to the bust in the Capitoline Museum. (Room of the dying Gaul no 9). Helbig thinks he perceives in this head the portrait of an eminent literary personage, probably Virgil. We, however, believe that it represents some personage of the imperial house of the Claudii.

26. Cippus found at Monte Mario. It belonged to the tomb of Minicia Marcella, daughter of C. Minicius Fundanus, Consul in 108 A. D. Pliny announces the death of this young girl in a letter to his friend Marcellinus (5. 16): thus;

« *Tristissimus haec scribo, Fundani nostri filia minore defuncta, qua puella nihil unquam festivius, amabilius, nec modo longiore vita sed prope immortalite dignius vidi. Nondum annos quattuordecim impleverat,* » etc.

Statoria Marcella whose death is recorded on the cippus no. 20 was probably her mother.

29. A Roman sarcophagus (2nd century) with a relief of the wedding ceremony of Creusa disturbed by the vengeance of Medea. On the left the children of Medea offer to Creusa, the nuptial gifts poisoned or enchanted by their mother; the veiled bride is modestly seated, and near her is her nurse who consoles her. Before her, on the left in an attitude of sadness stands Hymenaeus or Thanatos, a connection of two ideas which indicate that the marriage was destined to be unfortunate. In the middle is the principal scene, showing the results of Medea's vengeance. Creusa having put on the poisoned robes, is seized with madness, and springs frantically from the couch, while her aged father in desperation tears his hair. Then follows Medea meditating the murder of her children, who are unconsciously playing before her. Lastly, Medea in the chariot of the Sun drawn by winged dragons, carries away the corpses of her children. To the right of the sarcophagus are two heroes, perhaps Jason and Hercules, or Argus, discussing the Argonautic

expedition. On the left Iason (?) offers sacrifice. From the Caucci Palace, whence it had been removed to the Crypto-porticus of the Vatican.

This subject is often represented on sarcophagi, and another replica, with slight variations is no 49 on the 4th side of the garden.

30. Head of an unknown Greek portrait of the Hellenistic period. From the Kircherian Museum.

31, 33, 38 and 40. Fragments of a balustrade or parapet decorated with Victories striking down calves; a Roman work of the 2nd century of the Empire. Found in the Tiber near the Sublician Bridge.

32. Portrait, head of Domitian (?) From the Kircherian Museum.

37 and 41. Heads of telamones; the first represents Dionysos (Bacchus), the other Apollo. After the school of Pergamos.

Between the last two columns on the garden side, is a long block of marble divided into seven niches with columns, between which it is evident there once were statuettes. It was found in 1867 in the foundations of the Marignoli palace in the Via Convertite. As appears from the inscription on the back it belonged to a *spelaeum* or sacred grotto which Tamesius Augentius Olympius added to the sanctuary of Mithras built by his ancestor Nonius Victor Olympius « *caelo devotus et astris.* » This block probably dates from the years 382 to 391 A. D. The seven niches for statues refer, it is supposed, to the seven degrees of the mysteries of Mithras.

42. This and all the cippi arranged on the 2nd and 3rd sides of ihe garden were found in the course of the recent works on the banks of the Tiber The cippi were at unequal distances along the river, and served to mark the boundaries between the private property behind them and the public property which included the river and its banks. The most ancient are of the year of Rome 700, when two censors Servilius Isauricus and Valerius Messala fixed the limits of these lands; the most recent belong to the reigns of the Emperors Septimius Severus and Caracalla. They are useful in enabling us to determine the curves of the river, to establish the history of this portion of the Roman administration, and to give the names of the officials who took charge of it. One of these cippi found on the left bank of the river, behind the church of San Biagio della Pagnotta is of special importance as recording the existence of a *pons Agrippae* not otherwise known.

43. Beautiful Corinthian column of yellow African marble, from the Villa of Nero at Porto d'Anzio. Purchased from a dealer in Rome.

44 (Temporarily placed here). Colossal statue of an empress of the 1st half of the 2nd century. From the Sciarra collection.

CLOISTER 4th SIDE.

2. Statue wearing a toga. The body of the figure is on a grand scale; the ample flow of the toga indicates the fashion of the 3rd century; the head, which, evidently belonged to a statue of an earlier

period, is of the 4th or 5th century A. D. and ha
the incipient characteristics of Byzantine art, while
the style of the whole resembles the figures in mosaics and ivory carvings of the Christian period.
From the Platonia of St. Sebastian near the cata-
combs of San Calisto.

It stands on a cippus which contained the ashes
of three persons, among whom was Aurelia Nais,
dealer in fish near the grain stores of Galba.

3. Head of a woman contemporary with Julia,
daughter of Titus (b. about 39. d. 89 A. D).

4. Torso of Bacchus or of a satyr.

Opposite, under the arch, another torso of Bacchus after Praxiteles.

5. Head from the Via Ardeatina. Portrait of a
young Roman contemporary with Trajan. (98-117
A. D.).

6. Venus *Anadyomene* Cf. 2nd Side no 17.

7. Head of a Roman, period of decline of art.

10. One of the Muses. A statuette from Ostia.
It has been placed on a cippus from the Via Ostiense,
which belonged to a tomb made for himself and
his family by a freedman Calpurnius Chius who
was *sevir Augustalis* at Ostia, and held appoint-
ments in various institutions.

11. Fragment of a statue representing Hermes
(Mercury) a boy. From the Palatine,.

12. Pilaster decorated with fine bas-relief of
foliage.

From the collection at the Villa of Hadrian.

13. A bad replica of the head of Silenus from
the well-known group with the infant Bacchus (cf.
Museo Vaticano Braccio Nuovo no. 11).

15. Column intended to be placed on a spot granted by the curule aediles, as a support for a votive offering made by four magistrates of a village of which the name is not known. It was found in 1865, between the Via Labicana and the Via Latina whence it was brought to the Palatine.

17. Head of a man, of the end of the Republic or the beginning of the Empire.

Opposite. under the arch, fragment of a trophy with Corinthian helmet.

16, 19, 22, 24, 30, 34 and 38. Seven Hermes found in an *aedicula* near the Trastevere railway station are specially worthy of notice, for the delicacy of their execution, and the richness of the marble of their pedestals. They are portraits of charioteers of the first half of the 1st century A. D. In some of them the reins are twisted round the body (cf. the statue of the auriga in the Vatican Museum, Hall of the Biga N. 619; and the mosaics no. 9 Room XII.) They offer a considerable variety of ethnological types. The head of No 22 seems to have been made from a mask taken after death.

Opposite no. 19 under the arches are two fragments of sculpture of the later mediaeval period; i. e. a capital and a basin, the decoration of which is an imitation of Roman models. The inscription on the basin is curious: « *Hic Thetis, hinc esce, prius ablue, mande, quiesce,* » an exhortation to a guest to wash, eat, and repose. It bears the name of the artist: « *Magister Drudus me fecit.* »

G.

Two Rooms.

In the glass cases of these two rooms are exhibited specimens of barbaric industry, valuable not only for their workmanship, but also for the materials employed and for their great number. They were brought from excavations made under the direction of the curators of arts and antiquities at Castel Trosino near Ascoli Piceno where a cemetery has been discovered. Abont two hundred and fifty tombs have been opened, some of which were almost empty, others very rich in treasures. *

The tombs were rectangular pits covered merely with slabs of stone and placed according to the points of the compass without inscription of any sort.

In the first room are collected relics from the tombs of warriors, amongst which the set marked 119 (second and third glass cases,) especially remarkable for its richness, contains specimens of nearly all the objects in the other cases. In the middle of the lower division of the second glass case is the gold ornament for a saddlebow, decorated with lions heads of eagles, and dragons, and the so-called Lombard knots. The little bronze knobs are heads of nails with which it was fastened to the wood of the saddle. On the stand to the left

---

* Of similar character are the specimens bronght from Nocera Umbra, which are to be added to this collection, thus completing the series belonging to the barbaric civilisation of Italy.

is an iron dagger, of the sheath of which only the gold portions have been preserved: the rest, as in other objects in this collection was of leather, now destroyed. The cross was worn on the left shoulder. The small gold ornaments on the right in the last row belonged to leather tassels, the other ornaments were arranged on the dress. The heavy gold clasp weighs 52 grammes.

On the stand to the right of the upper case are arranged a pruning knife, a pair of shears and the point of a spear. The beautiful blue *rhyton* or drinking horn, as also the objects in the upper division in the next case, were found in the same tomb.

On the first stand is a rectangular piece of iron mail which was used for polishing horse armoou; on the second are an iron bit and spurs. In the middle of the third is the silver rim of a quiver, above are the frontal piece and the apex of a helmet, and the silver points of a bow, and at the sides triangular arrow-heads.

The dagger of tomb F, exhibited in the second case, is remarkable for the beautiful and characteristic decoration of the sheath.

In the first case are some articles made of iron inlaid with silver, found within the enclosure of tomb 9. In the two cases near the door are placed swords and plates of iron from cuirasses of the kind called *brigandines*, common at a later period, also four shields of which the leather portion has been restored. The size of these shields has been determined from that of the handles. The arm was not passed throngh, but the shield was grasped by the

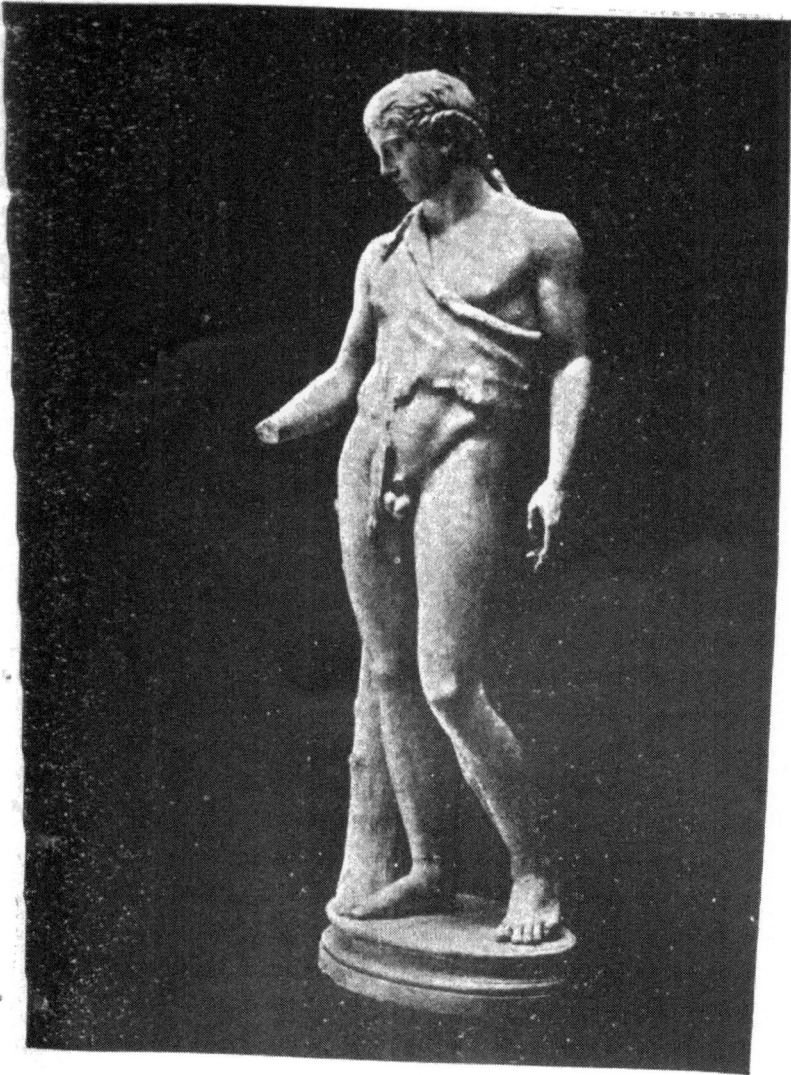

hand in the middle of the iron rib, so that the hand was protected by the boss.

In the second room are objects found in the tombs of women, many of them remarkably rich in ornament.

In nearly all were necklaces made of small globes or tubes of a many-coloured vitreous composition, sometimes varied with large crystals of quartz or coral beads, or more rarely with pieces of shells. This barbaric style of ornament strongly contrasting with the delicacy of the jewellery, was traditional up to the Lombard period, but it may be traced back to a very early date, examples of it being found in Egyptian and Phoenician tombs. It is perpetuated in the glass beads of Venice, which still find favour among savages.

In one of the necklaces of tomb 7 the vitreous beads are alternated with seven gold Byzantine *solidi* connected by an elegant twist of gold thread; in another with heartshaped pendants of gold; also in tomb 115 the necklaces are ornamented with Byzantine coins and pendants. From a necklace in tomb R hangs an amulet consisting of a pendant of transparent glass set with four bands of silver.

The large clasps of gold, two of which were found in tomb 1, served to fasten the dress on the bosom, and are the most splendid jewels of this collection. Scme of them are ornamented with beading and filigree work, others inlaid with vitreous enamel, others with carved gems of the Greek or Roman period.

The oblong *fibulae* (clasps) of silver, found always in pairs served to fasten belts. They are of the purest Lombard style usually ornamented with

4

beading, or with coloured glass. The gold and silver
rings are for the most part simple bands, frequently with two lozenges, perhaps to indicate conju-
gal fidelity. The gold and silver earrings are generally
large, with a hemispherical pendant, sometimes in
filigree; in some cases the pearl which ornamented
the back part of the disk has been preserved. Those
of tomb S. are especially rich and varied in form,
and have pearls and pendants of amethyst. The
crosses which were sewn on the dress are always
cut from a thin plate of gold, and are of the characteristic Lombard shape, (a Greek cross with
extended arms.) In tomb 32 the silver clasp is of
this shape, and bears the inscription: « Rustica
vivat. » In two of the tombs (nos 7 and 1) are silver ornaments like pins plated with gold, and with
pendants also plated with gold, fastened to the pin
with small chains.

The globes of rock crystal, (tomb 7 G.) terra-
cotta, or vitreous composition are weights used in
spinning. Some of them may be heads of pins for the
hair, or weights for tassels or cords. Of the combs
made of bone, found sometimes in the tombs, of
men, and in that case perhaps used for horses
manes, that of tomb 49 with a handle in which are
rounded hollows for the fingers, and that of tomb
22. on which is ronghly drawn a bird in the act of
pecking are especially worthy of notice. The three-
fold rings of tombs 13, 26 31 and 157 seem to have
been intended for fastening to the ribbons which
confined the hair like a net.

In the tombs of women were often found small
iron knives of which the silver portions of the
sheath are preserved. The custom of wearing a small

knife still prevails among the women of Norway.

Among the miscellaneous articles worthy of notice are the stirrups before-mentioned, (tomb 41) the chain and pin of which the head represents a centaur, (tomb 19) and the fibulae in the form of animals, of which the most characteristic is that of tomb 13 in the shape of a dove.

The terra-cotta vases and the glasses in these cases were found in the same tombs.

The beautiful gold fibula in case 5 was found in the stadium on the Palatine near the steps leading up to the imperial palace. It is thickly plated with gold, and ornamented with a double series of spirals with birds and a cross, a favourite idea of the Byzantine period. From its shape and decoration it is inferred that it was a work of the 4th century A D, and that it belonged to some court dignitary.

The marble ornaments on the walls of these two rooms were brought from mediaeval churches, and are of various epochs and origin, but from their style they belong to that Lombard or rather *Romanic* art which flourished from the 8th to the 12th century, and resulted from the grafting of barbaric and Byzantine elements on Roman art in its decline. They are similar in design to the barbaric jewellery, and have therefore been placed here.

In the first room, no 2 with two lions, was found near the Tiber. No 3 formed the front of an altar in the ruined church of San Flaviano in the valley of the Salino in the province of Teramo, not far from the district in which the rich tombs were discovered. It was presented to the museum by the Hon Giuseppe Cerulli. No 4 from a small collection. once kept in the University, is worthy of special

mention. It is of very barbarous art, and represents
a man grasping two dragons, an idea taken from
the classic legend of Hercules strangling serpents.

The relies in the second room are from the
church of S. S. Pietro and Marcellino on the Via
Labicana, except that opposite the entrance which
came from the *Xenodochion* of the Via Portuense.
They were all purchased from a Roman dealer in
antiquities.

CLOISTER. 4th SIDE CONTINUED.

Opposite No 22, the base of a tripod, decorated
with the attributes of Apollo, the crow, symbol of
prophetic power, the laurel, the bow and quiver,
the lyre, and the griffins.

25. Head resembling the Borghese Mars, attributed to Alcamenes (5th century B. C.). From the
Tiber.

26 and 27. Capitals from a small round temple
probably dedicated to Bacchus, the fragments of
which were found on the banks of the Tiber when
the Apollo Theatre was destroyed. The idea is new
and original; a tiger skin carved with great truth is
twisted round the capital. A fragment of the cornice
is no. 19 on the 4th, side of the garden.

H.

3. *Rooms.*

I.

4. Statue of Bacchus found in the Villa of Hadrian near Tivoli. A very accurate reproduction dat-
ing from the 1st century of the Empire of a Greek
statue in bronze attributed to Polycletus or to his

school. The original is one of the first attempts of
Greek art to give to the figures of certain masculine
divinities a feminine softness to express the effem-
inacy of their natures. Furtwaengler attributes it
to Euphranor, a sculptor who is considered to have
united the Peloponnesian and Attic traditions, and
who flourished between 375 and 330 B. C.

1. Head, portrait of Caligula (b. 10 BC. d. 54
A. D.) veiled as a sacrificing priest. From the Palatine.

2. Nero (b. 37 d. 68 A. D.) A head of great
character. From the Palatine.

3. Head of a woman, of the reign of Claudius.
From the Palatine.

5. Head, portrait of Livia (?) in advanced age.

6. Head, of about the time of Septimius Severus (?) (d. 211 A. D.). According to Helbig, it has
some of the characteristics of Clodius Albinus. (d.
197 A. D.). From the Palatine.

7. Head, one of the most beautiful portraits of
Antoninus Pius, (b. 86 d. 161 A. D.) cf. Room XI
no. 1. Purchased. From Formiae.

8. Very beautiful veiled head, portrait of Sabina,
wife of Hadrian (b. about 85 d. about 138 A. D.)
cf Room XI no. 10 and Cell F Room 2 no. 12.
From the excavations for the monument of Victor
Emmanuel.

2.

5. Apollo, a beautiful statue in Greek marble,
found in the Tiber, between Ponte Palatino and the
baths of Donna Olimpia in 1891. It is much worn
by the action of the water, yet in the outline of
the whole, and especially of the back, it displays

such grandeur of composition and of style that it is generally attributed to the youth of Phidias, though it may belong to an earlier period. Petersen believed it to be a copy of the work which Phidias executed for the Athenians, to be by them dedicated to the oracle of Delphi, as the tenth part of the spoil of the battle of Marathon. This was a group of Apollo with heroes, and Athena crowning the victor Miltades.

6. Athena (Minerva) a work of Doric art of the middle of the 5th century B. C. It seems to be original, and bears much resemblance to the statues on the pediments of the temple of Jupiter at Olympia. Found in the Tiber. The archaic rigidity of this statue contrasts with the softness of no. 4. which was originally on the Palatine, and was found in 1862 near the church of St Anastasia. It represents Charis, goddess of grace, or Aphrodite (type similar to the so-called *Venus Genitrix*) in the act of undressing; a graceful artistic conception of the time of Alexander the Great, known to us by many other examples, and by some attributed to Alcamenes.

2. Head of a dying Persian. A copy from one of the grand votive groups that Attalus I and Eumenes II, Kings of Pergamus had dedicated in memory of their victories over the Galatae. To these groups belonged also the so-called « Dying Gladiator » of the Capitoline Museum, the group of the Gaul and his wife of the Boncompagni Museum, the Amazons and Persians of the Museum of Naples and of the Vatican, and the Gauls of the Archaeological Museum of Venice. The nationality is indicated by the moustache, and by the tiara encircling the head.

In the face suffering and contempt of death in battle are powerfully expressed. Found on the Palatine.

3. Head of Venus, resembling the Cnidian Venus of Praxiteles. Found in the Tiber near Ponte Rotto.

7. Archaic Doric head of the 5th century B C. with abundant hair arranged in a curious point on the neck. It seems to be an original Greek work, and according to some it represents a Muse. From the Villa of Hadrian.

8. Head of the so-called Seneca, now believed to be Architas or Philetas of Cos, or Callimachus, or one of the poets of the later Hellenistic period cf. 1st Side no. 14. This is one of the best examples of the subject, and it is remarkable for the crown of ivy.

1 and 9 are two headed Hermes with the features of two divinities, one bearded, the other beardless. These Hermes served for decorations of gardens or to mark boundaries etc. cf. upper flooor Rooms I and VII.

3.

Contains statues found in the House of the Vestals (Atrium Vestae) in the Forum Romanum, portraits of priestesses, and especially of Vestales Maximae.

The statue no. 11 was found near a cippus dedicated to Flavia Publicia in 247 A. D.; it is therefore believed by some to represent that devout woman, but it seems more probable that this beautiful work of art was previous to the middle of the 3rd century, and might even be placed as early as the time of Marcus Aurelius. The figure which

wears the usual costume of a priestess prepared for
some sacrificial ceremony is carved with great artistic
accuracy and finish. As Vestal she is especially dis-
tinguished by the arrangement of her hair; she
wears a wig of which only the two front locks de-
scending to the ears are visible, perfectly distinguish-
able from the natural hair below; in other cases
where the head is uncovered the arrangement of
the hair suggests the *sex crines* (six locks) worn by
Vestals, and by brides on their wedding day.

Round the head are the six *infulae* (bands) the
ends of which fall down in front. The *suffibulum*
worn like a cap is represented in a somewhat unusual
manner; is is arranged to cover the head and drape
the neck, whereas in other statues of Vestals the
neck is covered by a separate garment; the medallion
which secures this kerchief is quite distinct from the
fibbia which fastens the suffibulum under the chin
in the reliefs of Palermo and Sorrento.

Nos. 4 and 10 represent a type of women grown
rigid in the life of the cloister. The head no. 3. seems
more antique; the *infulae* are arranged, Helbig says,
in imitation of the diadem style of hairdressing pre-
vailing under the Flavii. The others are portraits
of emperors and empresses who probably conferred
favours on the institution.

1. Lucius Verus (b. 130 d. 169 A. D.) cf 1st
Side 26.

2. Graceful head of Gordian III (b. 225 d. 244
A. D.).

5. Marcus Aurelius perhaps the best extant portrait of this emperor (b. 121 d. 180 A. D.)

7. Geta as a boy (cf. 1st Side 40).

8. Beautiful head, sweet in expression, a portrait of Lucilla (b. 147 d. 183 A. D.) wife of Lucius Verus (cf. Cell F. Room 3 no 2.)

9. Gallienus (b. about 220 d. 268 A. D.) very realistic head, and of fine workmanship.

11. Cararalla (b. 188 d. 217 A. D.).

CLOISTER 4th SIDE CONTINUED.

28. Sepulchral cippus in marble of Cantinea Procla, who from her dress seems to have been a priestess of Isis; in her right hand she holds a sistrum, and in her left a vase. On each side is the mystic cist.

29. Head of a barbarian of the Hellenistic period. It resembles in style and features the portrait statue of Mausolus, King of Caria (from 377 to 353 A. D.) brought to the British Museum from the Mausoleum of Halicarnassus. The decorations of this monument were by Scopas and his school. Opposite under the arch a fragment of a tripod of fine workmanship.

31 Head, portrait of a Roman of the 4th century A. D.

32 and 33. Pedestals or rather circular altars with the names of the goddesses Juno Lucina, and Minerva. From the Palatine. Under the arch a block of stone, centre of a fountain. The jet of water, falling on the little steps rebounded with a pretty effect.

35. Statuette of Telesphorus as a child. He wears a hood, and is seated asleep on a rock. From the Tiber.

38. Fragment of candelabrum with very delicate decorations in relief. Found at the Office of the War Ministry.

37. Angular front of a sarcophagus with a Medusa, very effective through the expression of suffering shown by the contraction of the face, and by the lines deeply carved in the dark marble. From the Tiber. (Mola de' Fiorentini).

39. Head larger than life, beautifully carved. It is a portrait of some great personage of the later Hellenistic period, or of the first century of the Empire. From the Tiber.

40. Statuette of Asklepios (Æsculapius) (cf. 1st Side no. 28). It stands on a cippus found at the Castro Prætorio, dedicated to the goddess Fortuna Restitutrix by a tribune of the sixth Praetorian cohort whose name has been effaced because his memory was condemned. The number of the cohort is also erased, but the word Maximinianae may be deciphered, and this determines the period (235-238 A. D.).

In the 4th Side are placed temporarily the marble blocks formerly in the courtyard of the Palazzo Fiano in Piazza San Lorenzo in Lucina. These formed part of the celebrated « ara Pacis Augustae » erected there in honour of Augustus on his return from having pacified Gaul and Spain (13 B. C). The fragment sawn into slabs and placed at the corner of the 3rd and 4th Sides, was recently found in the church of the Gesù where it had been used as a tombstone, as may be seen by the coat of arms of a bishop inlaid on the back. To fit it for this use the projecting portions of the relief had been barbarously chiselled away. Other fragments of this remarkable relic are in the Uffizi Gallery at Florence, in the Vatican Museum, the Villa Medici, and the Louvre. This altar was one of the richest and most beautiful examples of decorative art of the reign of Augustus. On the lower part is foliage designed with spirit and elegance, and above are encarpa suspended from bucrania forming a deep frieze.

The last block near the door has on one side an encarpus and on the other a portion of frieze representing a solemn sacrificial procession. The figures on this fragment are two attendants, one carrying the patera for offerings, and the praefericulum for libations, and the other driving a pig. Above is seen a temple with two seated divinities.

GARDEN SIDE I.

2. Central portion of a fountain in the form of a ship.

5. Hermes (Mercury). A repetition of the idea of the statue by Polycletus of a youth crowning himself.

12. Fragment of a statue of Tyche (Fortuna).

13. Colossal head of an empress of the time of the Antonines, perhaps Crispina or Lucilla.

14. Fragment of a statue of Artemis (Diana).

15. Seat for a statue, formed of piles of weapons.

19 and 20. Trapezophori i. e. supports for a seat.

24 and 26. Statues of Fortune.

25. A well head (puteal).

27. Pedestal of a statue erected in his own house to Volcatius Rufinus brother of Galla, and uncle of Gallus Caesar, related also to Volcatius Gallicanus, an author of the age of Constantine. He was consul in 377, praetorian prefect in 349 in which year he died. The cippus was discovered among the foundations of the Office of the War Ministry.

28. Sarcophagus with Cupids working at the vintage.

31. Sarcophagus with scenes of the chase.

32. A large base bearing a dedication to the Emperor Valens. It belonged to the arch forming the approach to the Valentinian Bridge (near Ponte Sisto). The other bases, intended for statues (no. 5 this side Side II no. 5) and the great marble slabs in the same row belonged to the parapet of the bridge.

46. Cippus belonging to the Julian, Tepulan and Marcian acqueducts at their junction.

49. Cippus referring to the redemption of public land through the *curatores locorum publicorum* of the reign of Tiberius.

51. Cippus belonging to the junction of the three acqueducts, (cf. no 46) erected by the curatores of the water.

52. Torso of Diana.

Garden Side II.

For the terminal cippi of the banks of the Tiber see Cloister 3rd Side no. 42.

5. Cippus upon which stood the bronze statue of Victory on the Valentinian Bridge (see upper floor room III no. 5.)

13. Torso of Diana.

16. Fragment of frieze with sacred emblems, a vase, *mensa* (table) with a *simpulum* (ladle), a *patera* (dish) a *pilus* with *apex*, the pointed cap of the *flamen*, *aspersorium* and a cymbal.

19. A telamon.

24. Torso of a nymph.

30. Torso beautifully carved, but much injured and worn away by the action of the Tiber. It represents Dionysos (Bacchus) style of Praxiteles.

32. Lattice.
45. Torso of Diana.
47. Portion of an antefixa.
52. Lattice.

GARDEN SIDE III.

1. Greek vase with heads of Ammon as handles.
13. Block of marble with inscription *di cava*.
24 and 25. Columns of cipollino found in the course of the demolition of the Apollo Theatre. Brought from the villa of the Gordians on the Via Appia.
26. Nymph with shell.
27. Half figure of Hercules.
31. Statue of Melpomene.
35. Tomb of republican period.
41. Sleeping nymph. Found near the Trastevere railway station.

GARDEN SIDE IV.

Fragment of a colossal relief, apparently the corner of a pediment on which is represented a figure of Ge (Earth) or one of the seasons. From the foundations of the Office of the War Ministry.
15. Centre of a fountain with water-jet. From the works on the Tiber near the Vicolo del Muro Nuovo.
19. Fragment of frieze of the shrine to which belonged the capitals nos 26 and 27 of the 4th Side (Cloister).
26. Sarcophagus with a concert of Cupids.
32. Torso of a statue of Hora (One of the Seasons).

36. Capital of grey granite in oriental or Byzantine style.

38. Capital in the form of a basket.

44. Sarcophagus with Cupids making arms at a forge (cf. Cloister 3rd Side no. 2.) From the Tiber near Ponte rotto.

46. Torso of Dionysos, (Bacchus) or a satyr. From the excavations for the monument of Victor Emmanuel (Via Giulio Romano).

47. Statue of Dionysos; style of the 4th century B. C. From the excavations for the monument of Victor Emmanuel.

49. Sarcophagus with scenes from the myth of Medea, formerly in the courtyard of the Reale Calcografia. (For the description see no. 29. 3rd Side of Cloister.)

ROUND THE FOUNTAIN.

Seven heads of animals used as water jets, sent here from the Kircherian Museum; previously in the Palazzo Valentini to which it is supposed they were taken from the Forum of Trajan.

Here also are some fragments of ancient mills in grey lava with the owners' names inscribed in cipher. They consist of a vertical cone (meta $\mu\acute{\upsilon}\lambda\eta$) round which revolved a stone hollowed to correspond, (catillus, $\H{o}\nu o\varsigma$) and pierced with holes for the insertion of a pole turned by an ass, a horse, or slaves, so that the grain was crushed by the friction.

Here too are large jars intended to contain grain, which show ancient repairs made with lead. From the *Cellae Arruntianae et Novae* near the Farnesina.

Towards the west is a wedge-shaped block of marble, bearing the name of Sentia, wife of Scribonius Libo, and mother of Scribonia, wife of Octavian. It was found in the Prati near the Tiber in front of the Casa Santini, at the eastern angle of the Piazza Cavour and opposite the new Palazzo di Giustizia.

The tomb on the north west of the garden originally stood near the Via Labicana, where it was difficult of access and exposed to risks on account of the works connected with the erection of the military railway-station of Tusculana, and because of the alteration of the acqueduct Felice. It was therefore taken to pieces, and re-erected here. It is constructed of tufa, with reliefs and inscriptions in travertine, and belongs to the last years of the Republic or the first of the Empire.

UPPER FLOOR.

On the staircase is a mosaic representing a libation From the Kircherian Museum.

Room I.

The marble fragments restored as two great pilasters were found in a wall constructed of heterogeneous materials in Via di Civita Vecchia, on the right bank of the Tiber opposite Santo Spirito, where the first pier of the new Ponte Vittorio Emmanuele stands.

On the first of these pilasters, to the right of the entrance, is an account of the secular games celebrated under Augustus in the year of Rome 737, (17 B. C.). It is the marble column which was erected in the *Tarentum*, the spot where the games

were held, in order to perpetuate the memory of
this solemnity, instituted to inaugurate the new
order of things.

This is an official report of the fifth celebration
in that year by command of the Emperor and the
Senate, and directed by the *quindecimviri sacris
faciundis* of whom the Emperor was one.

In order that the games might be performed
with due solemnity, the Senate decreed that all free
citizens must be present. The young unmarried men,
who were usually excluded from public festivals were
also to be admitted, because in the course of nature
they could never again see secular games. Women
were expected to leave off mourning attire, as
inconsistent with general rejoicing, and the tribunals
were to suspend their sittings.

From the 26th to the 28th of May the priests
were to purify the citizens who should present themselves with their wives and children; on the three
following days the Emperor or one of the other
quindecimviri was to receive the grain intended for
those who should take part in the ceremonies.

At the second hour of the night between the
31st May and the 1st June the sacrifices began on
the sacred spot in the Campus Martius which was
devoted to the secular games. On the first night
nine lambs and nine kids were sacrificed to the
Parcae; on the second loaves of various kinds were
offered to Ilithyia goddess of births, and on the third
a sow to Mother Earth. At the Capitol on the first
day two oxen were offered to Jupiter; on the second,
two cows to Juno, and on the Palatine on the third,
some loaves of bread to Apollo and Diana. The
matrons who were always present at these sacrifices,

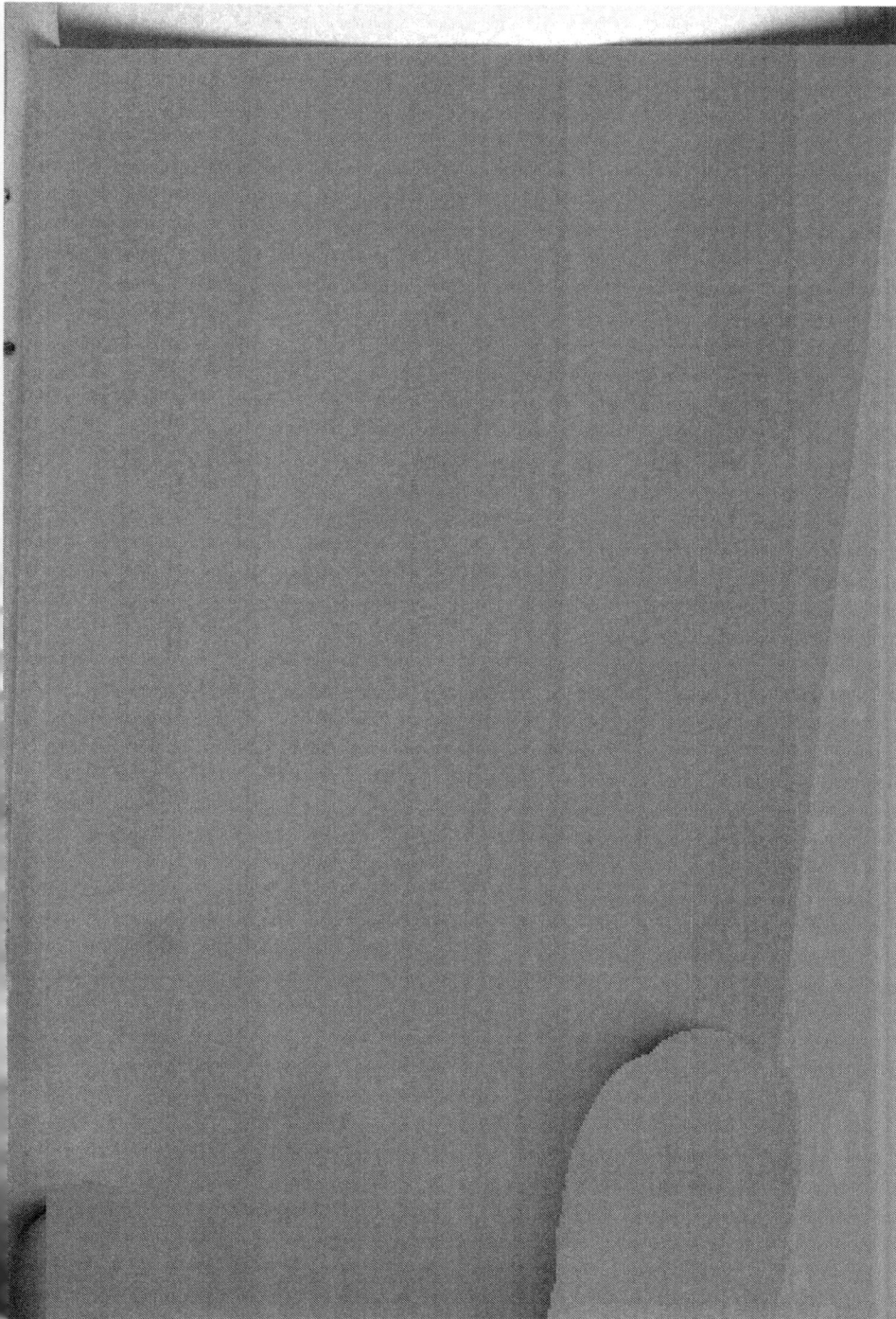

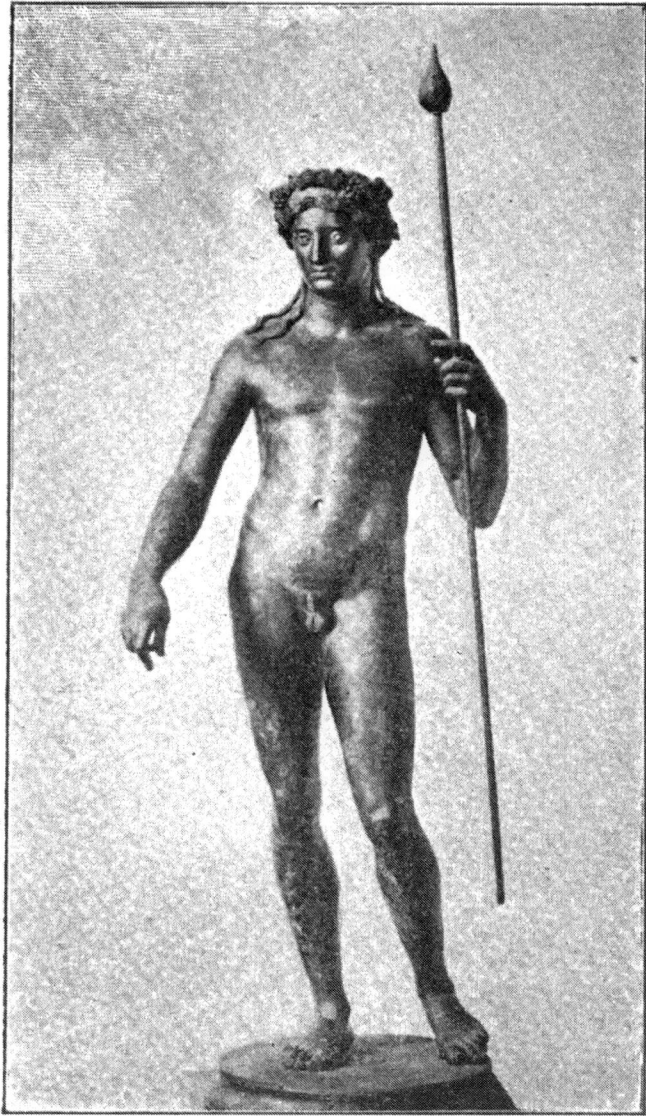

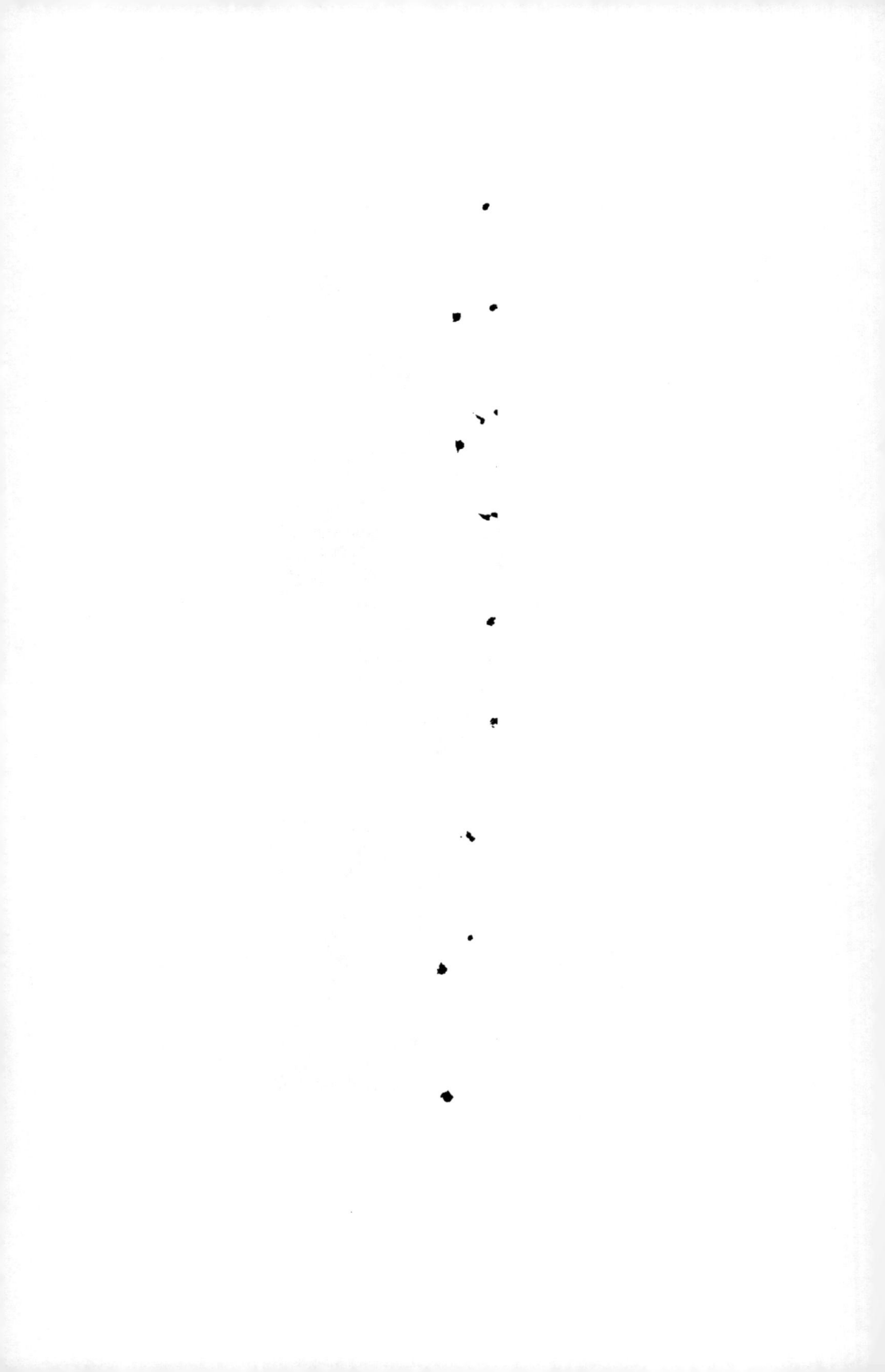

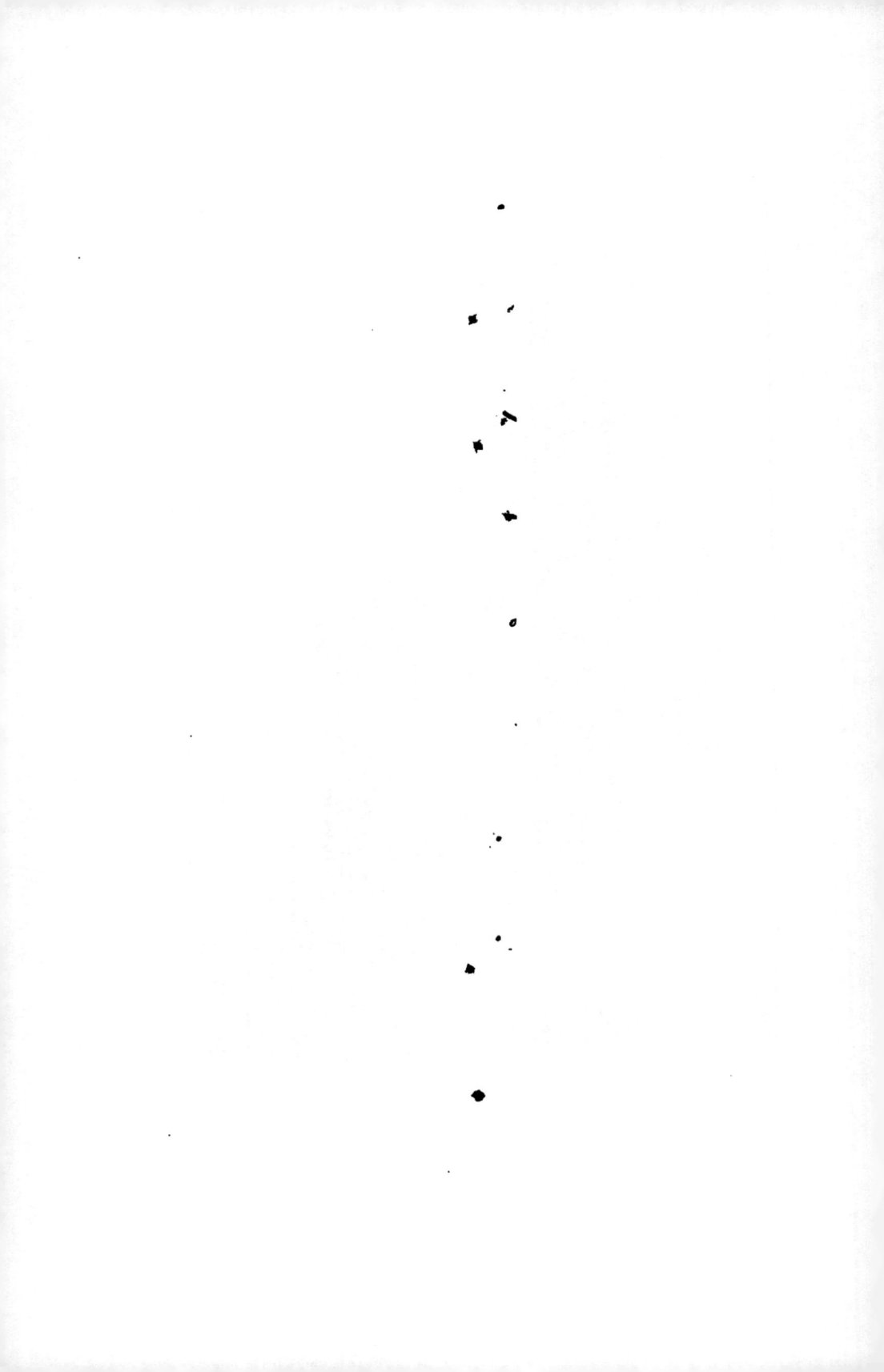

presided at night over the *sellisternia* (banquets)
offered to Juno and Diana.

Prayers were offered by Augustus and Agrippa,
not only in their capacity of *quindecimviri*, but also
as representing the new political and civil power;
by night the prayers were said by Augustus alone.

On the second day Juno as queen was invoked
by kneeling matrons, the number of whom was
equal to the number of years of the century. They
prayed the gods to increase the power and majesty
of the Roman people, to protect the Latin name,
to preserve it for ever unimpaired, safe and victorious, to favour the legions, to maintain the State
and to be propitious to the college of quindecimviri,
and to those who prayed, to their families and servants.

Besides the sacrifices, solemn games were begun
on the first night, according to ancient custom,
on a temporary platform; and these were continued
throughout the day; the Latin games were held in a
wooden theatre constructed near the Tiber, and both
were carried on for the two following nights and
days, then on the third day came the games of
the circus.

From the 5th to the 11th June other perform-
ances were given at the expense of the *quindecimviri*, — Latin games in the above mentioned wooden
theatre, in the theatre of Pompey Greek *thymelici*
i. e. plays performed in the orchestra, and in that
of Marcellus Greek *astici* or scenic plays. On the
following day a hunt in the circus, with perhaps
other circensian games, closed the festival.

Important as these details are in many respects,
it is yet more interesting to learn that on the third

5

day, at the conclusion of the sacrifice to Apollo and
Diana on the Palatine, twenty-seven boys and as
many girls sang on the Palatine, and afterwards on
the Capitoline, the famous song to the glory of
Rome and of Augustus, viz. the *Carmen Saeculare*
that we have all studied at school, written by Horace,
as line 149 on this marble tells us:

CARMEN. COMPOSVIT. Q. HORATIVS.
FLACCUS.

On the other pilaster is an account of the
seventh celebration of the secular games in the year
204 A. D. during the reign of Septimius Severus.
The sixth celebration had been held under Claudius,
and in this museum some fragments of the inscription
relating to it are exhibited in a frame in Cell D,
Room 3. no. 3. Of the inscription relating to the
seventh more than one hundred fragments have been
collected, and in the correct arrangement of them
the study of the Augustan inscription has materially
assisted. A few fragments of which the position has
not yet been decided, still remain, and may be seen
in Cell D, Room 3, no. 2. If the cippus of Severus
were less imperfect, we should have in it a record
of the greatest importance, because the festivals
and sacrifices were there described most fully and
minutely.

3. Fragment of a group of excellent Greek
sculpture, perhaps original. The subject has caused
much discussion; some maintain that it represents
Achilles supporting the body of Penthesilea, others
that it is the rape of Proserpine by Pluto, or one
of the Lapithae carried off by a centaur, or Nessus
and Deianira, or Boreas and Orithyia. Period of
Alexander or early Hellenistic. Found in the Tiber.

No. 5. A mosaic formerly in the Kircherian Museum, originally from the Via Appia (Convent of St Gregory, excavations by Tyszkiewicz). It represents a corpse almost a skeleton, pointing with the forefinger of the right hand to the highly philosophical inscription beneath: « Γνῶθι σαυτόν, » (Know thyself). The custom of representing skeletons in the triclinium, either on drinking vessels or on puppets to be placed on the table was the result of the preponderance of philosophical ideas at certain periods of Roman history; the object being to recall to the mind the brevity of human life, and to incite to the enjoyment of earthly pleasures.

No. 13. A marble slab on which are the rules of the bŭrial society of the worshippers of Diana and Antinous of Lanuvium, (Civita Lavinia) most important for the information it supplies respecting the organisation of such societies, the object of which was to secure to their members burial and funeral honours. It begins with a notice of the publication of the statute passed in the year 136, A. D. and an extract from a decree of the senate relating to those societies already authorised. Then follow the rules for the payment of entrance fees, the regulations for each month and for the funerals of members. Among other things it is directed that funeral ceremonies should be performed for those members who had been slaves, and whose bodies had been left unburied through the injustice of their masters. For suicides there were to be no funeral rites. There are also rules for banquets, for the management of the society, etc.

ROOM II.

The small but rich cinerary urns 1, 2, 3, 5, 7. 8, 9, of which the first three are overcharged with floral ornament, and the small bust no. 6 are from the tomb of the Platorini near the Farnesina on the bank of the Tiber, not far from Ponte Sisto. (Cf. cloister 1st Side, nos 1 and 3, and 2nd Side, nos 13, 19, and 25.). A water-colour drawing placed here shows the condition of the tomb when discovered in 1880. It is supposed that the beautiful young girl who was the original of the graceful bust no. 6 was *Minatia Polla* whose ashes are preserved in the urn no. 8 standing near. The tomb dates from the time of Tiberius.

Nos. 4 and 10. are portions of the vaulted ceiling of a room belonging to a house discovered in 1878 near the Farnesina. To this house belonged also the stucco reliefs and the paintings exhibited in Rooms V, VI, VII, VIII, IX, X and XI. It was a rich suburban villa of the reign of Augustus. The stucco reliefs of the vaulted ceilings are executed with great skill and freshness of touch; the only means used by the artist were a few free strokes of the modelling tool, or of the finger, and he thus attained a marvellous effect of chiaroscuro. The styles of ornament are various; in the different compartments are landscapes, winged Victories, half length figures of divinities, and scenes generally representing sacrificies to Dionysos, Priapus etc.

ROOM III.

Among the chief treasures of this museum are the two bronze statues nos. 2 and 6. found under the foundations of the Teatro Drammatico Nazionale

in 1884. No. 2 represents a personage with the attributes of a hero. Some believe it to be of the
Roman period, some of the Hellenistic; it is in the
same style as a statue of Alexander by Lysippus.
It is perhaps one of the Diadochi or successors of
Alexander, but the head being somewhat idealised it is
difficult to identify the features with those of any one of
them Some say it represents an athlete. The beard
is indicated by incised lines. The letters MAR are
pricked on the right thigh, and on the body L-VI-S(?)
L-XXIIX, which may refer to the original position
of the statue, or may indicate the weight of the
bronze. The idealised form of this statue contrasts
with the brutal truth of the other, which is however
more artistically perfect. It also belongs to the
Hellenistic period, and representes a pugilist at rest.
The profession may be inferred from the characteristics of the figure, the small cranium with diminutive
cerebral development, the face which is that of a
barbarian, the extraordinary muscular power in the
upper part of the body, the hairy skin, the ears
crushed by blows of the cestus. There are evident
tokens of recent combat, scars on the ears and
cheeks from which blood is trickling, the nose swoll-
en, and the weariness betokened by the elbows
resting on the knees. The cesti or padded gloves
studded with iron, and the *infibulatio* peculiar to
athletes, also denote the calling. On the right foot
is carved the letter A, a mark of the same kind as
that on the other figure. Some say that this statue
was dedicated by a victorious pugilist, and think
they recognise in it the Theban athlete Clitomachus,
who abont 200 B. C. conquered the Egyptian Arist-
onicus at Olympia, and during the intervals of the

combat roused in his own favour the patriotic feelings of the Greeks. It seems however, more probable that the statue formed part of a group in which we must imagine a wearied and defeated pugilist in conversation with his conqueror. The head is undoubtedly a portrait and recalls the features of the Farnese Hercules.

1. 4 and 7. Archaistic caryatids of Doric type in black marble. From the Palatine.

The bronze fragments nos. 3, 5 and 8 in this room as well as nos. 6, 8 and 9 of

ROOM IV.

Belong to bronze statues of Valens and Valentinian which stood on an arch that formed the approach to the Valentinian Bridge. They were found in the works for the Tiber embankment near Ponte Sisto. Here was also found no. 5, the wing of the Victory that stood above one of the pilasters of the same bridge. The pedestal of the statue and the dedicatory inscription found with the wing are now placed in the garden Side 2.

3. Statue of the youthful Bacchus in almost perfect condition. Though not remarkably beautiful in an artistic point of view, this statue is interesting for the fine and accurate workmanship of the details, especially the inlaying with silver and copper of the hair, lips, and breast, and the band round the head; the eyes are set in sockets. It is attributed to Campanian art of the 3rd. and 2nd. centuries B. C. On the calf of the left leg is fixed a coin which seems to be a Greek *didrachmon*. Found in the Tiber near the central pile of the Ponte Garibaldi on the 20th Sept. 1885.

7. A hand *averrunca*, ἀποτρόπαιον, i. e. a talisman against the evil eye. It was fixed on the bow of a ship. Found at the *Emporium* on the Tiber near the Marmorata.

1. Head in gilt bronze, a portrait of Tiberius (b. 42 B. C. d. 37 A. D.) From the Tiber.

2. Youth in green basalt, (this material was chosen to imitate bronze.) The head resembles a well-known bronze bust now in Munich, of Peloponnesian type of the 4th century B. C. Hauser says that this is a reproduction of one of the votive statues of athletes of the school of Polycletus dedicated in Olympia, and that it is a portrait of Glaucon of Dipaea. From the Palatine,

4. Bronze hermes, Roman style, representing Dionysos (Bacchus). From the Tiber near the Marmorata.

ROOM V.

* The two vaultings nos. 3 and 4 (B) (1) with reliefs in stucco contain a series of designs differing from those of the vaultings nos 1 and 6. (E).

The first (B) refers to Bacchic dances and the Dionysiac mysteries. e. g. in no 4. on the left is a scene of initiation; the second (E) contains mythological scenes.

The central relief in no 1. represents Phaethon accompanied by his pedagogue appearing before Apollo to ask if he is really his son; the god raises his finger in the act of swearing as he answers in the affirmative, and gives permission to Phaethon to drive the chariot of the Sun. On the opposite

---

(1) See plan hung in a frame in Room X.

relief though somewhat injured, the Hours and the Heliades are seen preparing the chariot for Phaethon. The rest of the decoration refers to the same subject; the caryatids are statuettes of divinities, — Jupiter, (Juno), Ceres and Mercury each occurring twice.

7. Vase from Hadrian's villa. Imitation of Alexandrine toreutic, — herons pecking serpents.

ROOM VI.

** In the middle a beautiful Greek statue found in the villa of Nero at Subiaco in 1884. By some considered to be an original, by others a copy from a bronze original. It represents a youth with rounded limbs, falling or in some other momentary action, hitherto unexplained.

It has been suggested that he is an archer, or one of the sons of Niobe, or Hylas escaping over sandy ground from the nymphs who pursue him, or Ganymede feeling himself seized by the eagle, a ball-player, a runner, a slinger, a thrower of the lasso, or a discobolus etc. A left hand holding a strap was found in the same place, but in spite of the resemblance of the marble, and even of the discoloration, it seems certain from the rough workmanship that it does not belong to this statue. In point of art the figure resembles the so-called Ilioneus of Munich, but its outlines are less accentuated, and therefore some believe it to be of later date (4th century B. C.); others refer it to the end of the 5th century, and believe it to be a work of Myron (Kalkmann).

The wall-paintings on a black ground marked C. are from the house near the Farnesina. These frescoes are similar to the so-called second Pom-

peian style, with a tendency towards the third or candelabra style. Observe the effect of aerial perspective obtained by means of columns and plinths in this and in similar mural decorations. On the frieze are depicted various scenes of misdemeanours, followed by trials in court. These trial scenes are not Roman in character but undoubtedly reproduce the costumes of the Hellenistic period. In all, the judge surrounded by his satellites is of regal aspect, while the accused and the litigants seem to be of low condition. Loewy conjectures that these scenes are taken from the anecdotes of the judicial life of Bocchoris, the wise king of Egypt, which were widely diffused in the ancient world. King Bocchoris was renowned for his astute decisions and his ingenious inventions to discover the criminal; he is what the wise King Solomon is to the Hebrew tradition.

These scenes cannot all be clearly explained, but we give the most probable interpretations of those best preserved. In the first on the left, a shepherd is watching a goat in a boat in the hope of stealing it, while another man carries off his; in the next the same men are disputing before the judge.

In the second picture three malefactors with hands bound behind them are led before the judge, whom three women endeavour to move to pity by throwing themselves on the ground before him weeping. In a preceding scene, which however is not very clear, a little fluttering Cupid shows that love is the cause of the crime. Here the three women appear occupied in a kitchen.

In the next scene a *res furtiva* is under discussion; a bundle is laid on a table before the judge, and three persons previously shown arguing in the open air are here continuing their dispute.

Next comes a comic scene; two men are quarrelling for a cloak; the younger tries to snatch it from the older, then both present themselves before the judge wrapped in the cloak to which both lay claim.

A man and a woman are quarrelling and the bystanders are trying to separate them; on the ground is a broken pitcher. Next, the same persons appear in court, but the connection with the preceding is not clear.

Then follow three villains illtreating a horse, whose owner hastens to appeal to the judge.

The introductory act is wanting to the next scene which recalls the famous judgment of Solomon. A soldier seems to be about to throw a child into a basin by order of the king while two women dispute, the one approving, the other in despair.

Another strange mode of trial is seen in the next picture. A man is held down in a bath, and a soldier is about to strike him, while a frightened woman tries to interfere. The next scene represents a man and a woman in excited conversation, while another woman, in terror, seems to be calling for help. The scene in court is perhaps a mode of trial invented by the judge in which the criminal reveals himself by his agitation. The means employed are not clear; three men are watching some small objects on the ground, two of them seem calm, and one excited.

When these walls were still fresh from the excavation the delicately executed landscapes on the black ground were still distinct, but of these only traces now remain.

In the recess of the large window are portions of the shafts of two columns of rare marble; one of bigio Africano, the other of breccia capitolina.

Small room A

Head resembling the well-known type commonly called Sappho, by some attributed to Silanion, an Attic sculptor of the first half of the 4th century B. C. It is more severe in aspect than the examples hitherto, known, and from the perfection of the work it might be believed original, and of more ancient date than that usually attributed to the replicas. Some say it is a poetess, perhaps Corinna, or a Muse or a Sibyl: the eyes are cast down in the act of reading or writing. The union of the real and the ideal in this head is worthy of notice, especially the contrast between the sensual fulness of the lips and the severity of the expression of the eyes, which gives it a character of individuality that may accord with the idea of Sappho. From the resemblance which it bears to the head on coins of Lesbos it may possibly be intended as a portrait of that poetess. From the stadium on the Palatine.

Small room B.

The best reproduction of the idea of the Hermaphrodite as seen in the statue of the Borghese Museum, and that of the Louvre. In this work of Hellenistic art, a graceful expression of a classic myth, the sculptor has sought to unite the attractions of both sexes, and by means of sleep to give a character of softness to the figure. That this sleep is not quiet and natural in apparent from the disarrangement of the drapery by the motion of the foot and arm. From the foundations of the Costanzi Theatre where it was

discovered in 1879 on the spot on which the house
of Julius Avitus grandfather of Heliogabalus is supposed to have stood.

ROOM VII

In this room are paintings marked B. from one
of the bedrooms of the house near the Farnesina
showing a union of various styles and of different
periods. In several cases there seems to be an
intentional contrast between opposing styles. The
picture on wall no. 4 executed with much truth and
realism rivals modern fresco painting both in composition and colouring. The subject, which is intended to appear as though seen through a window,
is the nymph Leucothea nurse of Dionysos (Bacchus), holding the child on her knee and adorning
his head with vine-branches, while Semele, pleased
at seeing her son in such loving care, looks on
from the back ground.

This naturalistic scene is placed between two
others representing framed pictures against a wall,
supported by decorative figures and painted in archaistic style in imitation of the Greek paintings
of the 5th century B. C. especially those on the
Attic vases called *lekythoi.* In these pictures are
represented girls playing on musical instruments;
on the strings of the lyre are inscriptions, and this
detail is imitated from the above mentioned vase
paintings.

The large central picture of wall no. 5 in the
same style represents the toilette of Aphrodite
(Venus) with Eros (Love) holding her sceptre, and
a Χάρις (Grace) who is arranging her veil on the

polos (a kind of crown shaped like a basket, Lat. *modius*).

The paintings on the frieze refer to theatrical episodes or love scenes, and are represented as though provided with small doors. The decorative figures on the walls, and indeed all the designs are suggested by Egyptian, probably Alexandrian models.

1. This beautiful head is an Asklepios (AEsculapius) of the second Attic school, after the Olympian Zeus of Phidias. It belonged to a colossal statue found on the Palatine, of which the feet and the base are also preserved here.

4. A pleasing portrait of a Roman girl, unknown. Observe the peculiar arrangement of the hair. From the Palatine.

In a case in the middle of the room are glass vessels found at Campagnano, and a cup of Arretium ware found at Civita Lavinia with reliefs referring to the worship of Mithras of which it is one of the most ancient proofs in Italy.

The small glass bird, a child's toy, intended to float on water, was found with some coins of Domitian in a tomb at Rondissone near Alessandria in Piedmont.

ROOM VIII.

In the case in the middle are various bronze objects, among which a scraper (strigilis) found in the Tiber, a *sistrum* or rattle used in the worship of Isis, and a beautiful bronze helmet which was perhaps in the hands of the statue of Victory on the Valentinian Bridge. (cf Room IV no. 5.) Among some cups from Arretium are placed small but elegant models of furniture and domestic utensils made of lead, probably children's toys given as votive offerings.

They were found in the excavations of the, supposed site of the temple of Jupiter Anxur at Terracina, and dedicated to Jupiter as a child; or perhaps offered by brides before marriage in the temple of Venus.

In the upper division of the same between a bronze statuette in the style of the famous Doryphorus of Polycletus and one of the Lares, is a guest's token, shaped like half of the head of a ram, and inscribed with the names of two persons bound by links of hospitality, who each possessed one half of the head.

1. Head of Apollo, style of 3rd century B.C.

4. Head of a boy smiing, very sweet in expression.

The pictures in this room from the same house as those already described, show, like them, a contrast of styles: some in the archaistic manner before mentioned, deserve special consideration for their grace and delicacy of execution (nos. 6, 8, and 9.) No 9 is a simple drawing of a girl pouring an unguent from a bottle into an ointment box. (*alabastron*).

* 10. Roman head, portrait of an adult without hair or beard, of the later republican period. Important for simplicity of modelling and for the ethnological type. (cf Cloister 3rd Side, no. 23).

Found in the Tiber.

ROOM IX.

These paintings which are from a sleeping room in the same house as in Room VIII, display the

contrast of styles already noticed. The subjects and
designs though quite different, are not original; in
some of the squares forming part of the decorations
are figures on a dark ground recalling the graceful
statuettes of Tanagra, others represent *pinakes* or
pictures hung on walls, of which some are love
scenes in Hellenistic style.

On the portion of wall marked D. I. on the
second column to the right is inscribed « Σέλευχος
ἐποίει » perhaps the signature of the artist.

5. Head of Antinous as a youth. From Hadrian's villa.

In the middle of the room is a triangular base
for a candelabrum with three figures in relief representing Apollo Lycius or Palatinus, a priest
(quindecimvir?) carrying a basket with offerings, and
Ceres, (?) or perhaps a Sibyl. The candelabrum
may have been connected with the worship of A-
pollo Palatinus, and with the sibylline books which
were preserved in his temple under the care of
quindecimviri sacris faciundis. From the neighbourhood of the Baths of Titus.

ROOM X.

The female head near the window was found
in the villa of Nero at Subiaco. It is that of.
a girl sleeping in the usual position of the statues
called ἀναπαυόμεναι and recalls the celebrated
statue of Ariadne in the Vatican (Gallery of statues
no. 414.) This head excels others of the same subject in delicacy of execution and the sweetness of
the expression of the eyes and lips as well as in the
truthfulness of the waving hair. It suggests to the

mind the verses of Propertius who compares his
sleeping love to a statue of Ariadne:
« *Talis visa mihi mollem spirare quietem*
Cynthia non certis nixa caput manibus. »
The original of this work belongs to the 4th
century B. C. The hollow on the head was intended
to support the arm which rested upon it, and was
separately carved.

On the wall is a plan of the house near the
Farnesina. The paintings here exhibited once adorned a corridor of this house; a portion large enough
to show the whole scheme of decoration is preserved, and also some of the central pictures
though so much injured that it is difficult to explain
the subjects.

In the middle of the other painting no. 22. is
a rural scene roughly sketched, in which a traveller
makes an offering before a bronze statue of Athena
Promachos raised on a pedestal. At the sides are
two majestic figures of Muses of a severe type of
beauty and full of expression.

ROOM XI.

In two glass cases in the centre is a collection
of Roman and Byzantine coins (*solidi aurei*) found
recently in a subterranean chamber under the House
of the Vestal Virgins on the slope of the Palatine.
This chamber was approached by a flight of four
steps, shut off from a corridor by a trap-door. The
coins had been concealed by some one who had fast
ened them up in some perishable wrapping, pere-
haps a bag or handkerchief, of which not a trace remained. The most ancient coin dates from Costan-

tine II (323-351 A. D.) two are of Lybius Severus,
(461-465 A. D.) eight of Marcianus, (450-457 A. D.)
345 of Anthemius, (467-472, A. D.) ten of his wife
Euphemia, and twenty four of Leo I (457-474 A. D.).

The paintings on a white ground decorated
another corridor of the Farnesina house. On the
frieze are landscapes alternating with masks and
other theatrical properties. The landscapes are important as having Egypto-Hellenistic characteristics.
In G. 1. is a naval battle in a harbour; G. 2. and
F. 2. fishing scenes, G. 3. buildings and shrines,
statues and altars; F. 2. on the right an offering
to Mercury, a scene similar to that described in
Room X, with city gates, a market etc.

1. Bust in beautiful Parian marble, a portrait of
Antoninus Pius (cf. H. Room 1, no. 7). From the
stadium on the Palatine.

3. Sabina (cf. H. Room 3, no. 12). From the
Via Appia·

10. Head of a woman of the time of the later
Antonines.

13. Head of an unknown personage of the
early Empire.

ROOM XII.

The coins in central case were ·found in a jar
hidden in a corner of · the atrium of the House
of the Vestals in a room built during the middle
ages. The jar was found during the excavations
made in 1883 under the ministry of His Excellency Guido Baccelli, and the coins were examined and explain-

ed by the illustrious De Rossi. A catalogue is hung on the wall. They are 835 in number; the only one of gold is a solidus of the Emperor Theophilus (820-842 A.D.). Of the silver coins 830 were stamped by the Anglo-Saxon kings at their own mints; two are from Pavia, one of which bears the name of the Emperor Berengarius (915-924 A.D.) the other bears the monogram of Hugo and the name of Lotharius both kings of Italy (931-946); one is from Limoges with the stamp of the coins of Eudes king of France (888-898) and one from Ratisbon with the stamp of Duke Arnulph (912-937.).

The Anglo-Saxon coins, for the most part clear and sharp, belong to Alfred the Great (871-900 A. D.), Edward the Elder (900-924), Athelstan, (924-940). Edmund I (944-946), Sitric of Northumbria, (914-926) Anlaf of Northumbria (927-944), Plegmund, Archbishop of Canterbury (889-923).

The double clasp found in the same jar is ornamented on the outer side with a trifolium inlaid in silver surrounded by a double line, within which are the letters « † DOMINO MA » on the one half and « † RINO PAPA » on the other; probably referring to Pope Marinus II, contemporary with Anlaf and Edmund I. The clasp served to fasten on the shoulder the *cappa pluvialis*, a large cloak worn by pontifical officers and soldiers, and as no other similar clasp has come down to us with the name of the reigning pope, it is probable that this belonged to one of the great dignitaries of the papal court, perhaps to a *vestiarius* (keeper of the wardrobe) and of the money kept in reserve.

The great number of different names of mints and masters of mints on the reverse of the coins

indicates that they must have been collected one by
one, and from house to house throughout the island.
The fact of the clasp having been found in the
same vessel goes to prove that these coins are the
oldest instance of *Romscot, Romfeah, Romepeny,
Rompening*, a money contribution instituted towards
the close of the 8th century or the beginning of
the 9th. This was exacted from every head of a
family possessing a certain quantity of land, and
was devoted to the maintenance of the *hospitium*
of the Saxons in Rome, and to the oblations made
to the basilicas of the apostles and to the pope.
The pontifical official may have received his ho-
norarium in coins of this tribute, or he perhaps had
charge of the money and concealed it for the ex-
penses of the war with Hugo, king of Italy.

The apparently strange discovery of mediaeval
coins in the House of the Vestals may be explained
by the fact that Pope John VII, who was born and
brought up in the ancient *Palatium* began to build
a house for himself and his successors on the slope
of the Palatine towards the Via Sacra. This house
never was finished, but the site remained in the
possession of the Roman Curia.

1. Head of Socrates. From the excavations for
the monument to Victor Emmanuel.

3. Greek portrait, 5th century. Copy of a bronze
original.

* 8. Greek youth; the expression of the features indicates fear. Style of 4th century B.C. According to Helbig, it probably belonged to a group
in which Scylla is seizing one of the companions
of Ulysses (cf. Museo Chiaramonti of the Vatican,
no. 79).

10. A beautiful head, the face singularly animated and satirical in expression. It is said to be a portrait of one of the Diadochi or successors of Alexander the Great. (cf Cloister 3rd Side n. 17.).

Mosaic.

2. A very fine mosaic with figures of Victory. From a villa at Tusculum excavated in 1841.

The other mosaics are from a villa of the 2nd or the beginning of the 3rd century of the empire; it stood at the 17th milestone on the Via Cassia, near the estate called *Ad Baccanas* where Caracalla and Geta had property.

4. a. Ganymede carried off by the eagle.

4. b. Philoctetes ?

4. c. Ulysses escaping from Polyphemus.

4. d. Pastoral scene.

5. a. Aphrodite (Venus) with the swan, or Hebe with the eagle of Jupiter.

5. c. A river scene.

6. Four of the Muses.

7. a. Bacchus disputing with the Indians. From Tusculum.

9. The four figures of charioteers each leading a horse represent the four factions of the circus with their distinctive colours: *albata*, white; *russata*, red; *prasina*, green; and *veneta* blue. They wear their characteristic costume, a coloured tunic over which the reins are twisted, gaiters to defend their lower limbs, and knee-caps to prevent the knees from being rubbed by the sides of the chariot.

11. Love seizing Pan by one of his horns.

12. A Flora or Spring, tasteless in design, but fine workmanship.

ROOM XIII.

The paintings here are much injured, and one
of them has been scraped with a view to covering
the wall with fresh plaster. They were found in a columbarium near the tomb of the slaves and freedmen
of the Statilii, in the neighbourhood of the Porta
Maggiore. From the same place were brought the
three portraits in travertine nos. 1, 2 and 3. These
four paintings adorned the walls of the sepulchral
chamber, forming a frieze above the niches for the
urns. They are important not only from an artistic
point of view, but also from their subjects. From
the style of the tomb and of the paintings and inscriptions, it has been inferred that they belong to
the age of Augustus. They represent scenes in the
myth of Æneas and his successors up to the time
of Romulus, for the most part connected with the
foundation of the three Latin cities, Lavinium, Alba
Longa and Rome. With these are grouped various
subordinate scenes and episodes of the legend in
chronological order. Under the purple border are a
few lines written in black ink which though now
hardly legible have aided in the explanation of the
subjects. It is worthy of notice that excepting the
meeting of Mars and Rhea Silvia, every mythological and supernatural element has been excluded
from this series of paintings, which, natural and
realistic as they are, may be said to form a pictured
chronicle. The artist in planning his work was doubt-
less guided by the legend as it was treated in the
reign of Augustus, and especially by the style of
the paintings which were carried in triumphal pro-

cessions, and which represented historically the e-
vents and circumstances of the long war or expedition conducted by the victorious general honoured
by the triumph.

21. - I. Foundation of the city of Lavinium by
Æneas. Two towers and part of the wall are seen,
upon which five workmen are engaged, while two
others carry squared stones. At the foot of one of
the towers is a woman, the personification of
the city.

II. Battle at the river Numicius between Latins and Rutulians. Two warriors lie dead. The
Latins may be recognised by their complete armour,
viz. lance or sword, cuirass, helmet, and *clipeus* or
round shield; the Rutulians are naked and carry
rectangular shields.

21. - III. Æneas having struck down Turnus,
king of the Rutulians, is crowned by Victory who
approaches with a palm in her left hand, a crown
in her right. Æneas wears a tunic and cuirass, and
carries a shield; at his feet the prostrate figure of
Turnus is indistinctly seen.

IV. Another battle at the Numicius. This scene
begins with the group to the left of Æneas, and
terminates with the nude figure of a soldier holding
a purple cloak fluttering from his left arm; he
poises himself on his left foot, and raises his right
hand in act to strike. The beauty of the composition and the animation of the group of warriors,
one of whom falls pierced by a lance in the shoulder, are worthy of notice.

V. Flight of the Rutulians defeated by the Latins, one of whom, a powerful warrior wearing a cuirass and a plumed helmet, advances on the left.

The bearded and crowned figure in the middle, seated on the ground and holding a reed in his left hand, represents a river god.

VI. Peace. Two enemies who having placed their shields behind them and pointed their lances towards the ground, join hands, while in the background at a distance are seen witnesses of the reconciliation.

VII. Foundation of Alba Longa. While one workman raises what seems to be a spade to fill a basket with earth, another with his back turned lifts a basket already filled, and a third stoops to lift another. Their companions collect and carry stones for the walls under which sits the personification of Alba Longa wrapped in a long purple cloak over a green χιτών, with a mural crown on the head.

VIII. Ascanius gives up Lavinium to his mother (?) This scene perhaps alludes to the legend, that after the death of Æneas, his son Ascanius went to live at Alba Longa, giving up Lavinium to his mother Lavinia. Ascanius is standing and a seated woman, half naked, probably a nymph (Egeria?) addresses him. Near her, attended by two maids, sits another woman, crowned, in a mournful attitude, the personification of the city.

20. - IX. Rhea Silvia becomes a Vestal. Among a group of girls the prominent figure is Rhea Silvia, wearing a reddish χιτών and a long white veil, with a sad expression, resting her hand on the shoulder of her mother or of her cousin Antho. As the daughter of Numitor she is destined to become a Vestal, but her father, seeking to save her from her fate addresses his brother Amulius,

who is seated on his throne wilth his daughter Antho behind him.

X. Rhea Silvia is surprised by Mars. Two shepherds are running away, frightened at the sight of the war-god, who draws the Vestal towards him, while Victory who never forsakes him, takes off the maiden's cloak. From her hands falls the pitcher with which she had gone to draw water.

Fortune, the friend and mistress of the Roman people, stands by, holding a cornucopia. Beside her sits the personification of a stream.

XI. Condemnation of Rhea Silvia. Seated on a throne, king Amulius pronounces sentence of death on Rhea Silvia who sits mournfully on the right of the picture. On the left, also seated, is the unhappy father Numitor, who is declared to be the accomplice in the crime. Behind are two men sadly watching the scene.

19. XII. Punishment of Rhea Silvia (?) Of this scene only two figures remain, on the right a youth, on the left a woman seated on a rock. This picture may represent the last moments of the Vestal who was thrown into the Tiber.

XIII. Romulus and Remus about to be exposed in the Tiber. The river-god armed with an oar to show that the Tiber is navigable, extends his right hand as if in invitation or protection to two servants who carry the twins in a flat basket.

XIV. Romulus and Remus as shepherds. The twins, fully grown, lead the sheep to the pasture while a local deity nearly effaced from the picture, is seated on a hill to the right as their protector. The figure of the young shepherd on the left is natural and full of beauty. .

The beginning and end of the frieze have been
lost. The first scene was perhaps the arrival of
Æneas in Latium or his meeting with king Latinus,
or the betrothal of Æneas. The last was probably
the foundation of Rome.

The fragments 10 and 11 deserve special consideration as beeing exquisite examples of decorative
painting. Observe especially in no. 10 the face of
a woman with a nimbus, in no. 11 the girl carrying a burden on her head, and the woman seated
in a pensive attitude. Small as this last figure is
the eyes are full of penetration.

In nos. 8 and 11 on a polished black ground
are flowers, fruit and birds which for truth and
delicacy will bear comparison with the best specimens of similar subjects in Japanese art.

The other paintings are fading. No 3. Fortune
with the nimbus, was found at the now levelled
Monte della Giustizia which was near the railway
station.

7. According to Helbig, this represents Scylla
carrying to Minos the lock of hair.

In the middle of the room are specimens of
glass rendered iridescent by oxidation, so as to
equal mother-of-pearl in beauty, the greater number of which were brought from the tomb of the
Statilii. Among these may be seen two small earthen
vases, glazed or covered with vitreous enamel,
rare examples of an art not fully developed in classic times. They are of the first century of the Empire, and are from the Palatine.

The small statuette near the door is a sin-
gular example of technical skill and patience,
executed as it is with the utmost delicacy in hard

basalt; the details of the drapery, the hair, and the ornaments of the tripod on which the figure is seated are especially remarkable. It is perhaps copied from a bronze original representing a Pythia. From the Tiber near the Ponte Garibaldi.

12. A finely wrought cinerary urn, also found in the tomb of the Statilii. The bas-relief represents a scene of initiation into the Eleusinian mysteries, not those of Eleusis in Greece, but those that were celebrated near Alexandria. The person to be initiated sits upon the mystic *cista* which is covered with a skin. His head is veiled, and he holds a torch which rests on his left shoulder. Behind him a *hierodula* or attendant priestess passes over his head the λίχνον or mystic winnowing fan, symbol of purification, while on the right the priest is in the act of pouring a libation over the pig held on the altar by an ἐπιβώμιος or assistant, wrapped in a skin. The principal divinities of Eleusis are present; Demeter (Ceres), Kora (Proserpine), and Triptolemus caressing a serpent, the symbol of divination.

This urn is copied from a metal original, cast in the Alexandrine period.

ROOM XIV.

The beautiful sarcophagus exhibited here is from the tomb of Calpurnius Piso on the ancient Via Salaria. (Villa Bonaparte). It is worthy of notice as having been left unfinished and used in this state with the addition of a rough cover. The scene on three of its sides is remarkable for animation and freshness of touch, and for harmony of composition:

it is the thiasos or cortège of Bacchus performing
orgiastic dances, the scanty garments of the Maenads
fluttering with their wild contortions. A drunken
Silenus leans on a satyr; Pan plays with a goat
showing it a bunch of grapes towards which the
animal looks eagerly and springs. Satyrs and Maenads dance wildly round the altar of Dionysos,
the mystic *cista* and the masks, to the music of
cymbals, tambourines and pipes.

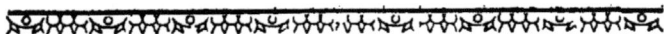

ALTERATIONS AND ADDITIONS

MADE DURING PRINTING

—∿∿∿—

4. Now placed in Cell F, 3, n. 3. In its place: Head of an aged Roman matron veiled, of the time of the Antonines. From the Tiber.

14. Formerly numbered 19.

15. Similar to the preceding, but more finished. From Civita Lavinia.

18. Now in Cell F. 3 n. 6. — In its place n. 11 of room F. 1.

19. Formerly numbered 14.

37. Now in the garden, Side 1. In its place: Colossal headless statue of Fortuna or Abundantia, or of a Roman empress with the attributes of these deities. The arm shows traces of a cornucopia. Found near the office of the Ministry of Agriculture.

2nd SIDE.

4. Now in Cell F, 3 n. 1. — In its place n. 22.

CELL B.

At the entrance a statue of Bellona on a throne supported by two lions.

Room 1.

n. 3. Now in room 4. In its place n. 5 ot room 3.

Room 2.

Styles of hair-dressing fastrionable among Roman ladies under the Empire. Formerly in Cell F Room 3.

Room 4.

3 of room 1 and n. 2. 7 of room 3.

Porch.

n. 1 Torso of a male statuette resembling the Ludovisi Ares.

n. 2. Statue much worn away, evidently Eros from the holes in the shoulders for wings. Style of the 4th century B. C.

2nd SIDE CONTINUED

12. Formerly 1nd side n. 4.

18. Bust of a Roman boy; From a columbarium on the Via Ostiense.

CELL D.

Room 2.

Mithriac sculptures.

Room 3.

The statue of Hermes now placed in Cell F. 3.

Porch.

Headless statue of an old woman with a vase, resembling another figure carrying a lamb in the Palazzo dei Conservatori. A mediocre copy of an original of the Hellenistic period. Much damaged. From Sutri.

2nd. SIDE CONTINUED.

Between 21 and 22. Cippus with a figure of Silvanus, dedicated by the *equites singulares*.

22. Portrait of Socrates (cf Upper floor, Room XII no. 1). From the Via Latina.

CELL E.

Room 3.

Under no. 3. Part of a puteal decorated with bas-reliefs representing three Maenads in the distorted attitudes of an orgiastic dance, according to a favourite idea in Neo-Attic bas-reliefs. Fine execution. From the Sciarra Collection.

CELL F.

Room 1.

In the places of nos. 8-11:

3. Formerly in Room 2.

9. Torso of the Minotaur struck down by Theseus; fragment of a group in excellent Greek sculpture, copied from a bronze original of the 5th century.

Of the Attic school, perhaps from the studio of one of the sculptors of the Parthenon. Note the vigorous muscles skilfully modelled in a style resembling that of Myron, the ability with which the artist has expressed both human and animal force, and the life which breathes from every part. Found together with the following fragment of the same dimensions and of the same marble, in the garden of the hospital at San Giovanni in Laterano.

10. Torso of a youth bending forwards. At first supposed to be a torso of the Theseus stricking down the Minotaur, and with this view the restoration was attempted, but the difference of style in the two torsos seems to contradict this hypothesis. The softer and less animated modelling of the youth contrasts with the energy expressed in the Minotaur. Found with the preceding in the garden of the hospital at San Giovanni in Laterano.

11. Head of Apollo of the type known as the Apollo Choiseul-Gouffier. Archaic style of the 5th century B. C.

Near the entrance. Cinerary urn bearing an inscription apparently substituted for another previously erased. On the urn is the story of Pasiphae in relief with the unusual additions of Daedalus and a Cupid. Representations of this legend are very rare, especially in sepulchral monuments.

Room 2.

In the middle. Torso of a nated youth, an excellent copy of a Greek statue of the 5th century. The most perfect copy is in the British Museum. It is believed to represent Cyniscus of Mantinea as victor in a boxing match in the act of placing a

crown on his head: a work of Polycletus, the base
of which was discovered at Olympia.

4. Head of a beautiful youth, evidently Pan
from the small horns. Attributed to Polycletus.

Room 3.

Statue of Hermes, formerly in Cell D. 3.
1. formerly 2nd side n. 4.
2. formerly 4nd side n. 11.
3. formerly 2nd side n. 2.
4. formerly 3nd side n. 17.
6. formerly 1nd side n. 18.
7. formerly 2nd side n. 18.

Small Room 4.

Archaistic statues of a man and woman, one the
pendant to the other. The head of the man and
part of the breast are modern. — From the Sciarra
Collection.

2nd SIDE CONTINUED.

32. Head of a Roman. — From a columbarium
on the Via Ostiense.

3rd SIDE.

17. now in Cell F. 3. n. 4. — In its place
n. 10 of room F. 1.

4th. SIDE.

11. now in Cell F. 3 n. 7. — In its place n. 9 of
room F. 1.

9 781021 187758